REPOWERING AMERICAN INDUSTRY!

Together We Can Compete in a Global Economy

BRUCE J. KNIGHT

Copyright © 2009 Bruce J. Knight
Permission to reproduce or transmit in any form or by any means, electronic or mechanical, including photocopying and recording, must be obtained by contacting Bruce J. Knight at e-mail brucespeaks@knightgates.com.
All rights reserved.

Editor: Nicole Walsh

ISBN: 1-4392-4140-6
ISBN-13: 9781439241400
Library of Congress Control Number: 2009904777

To order additional copies or arrange a speaking engagement, visit www.knightgates.com or send an e-mail to brucespeaks@knightgates.com

Dedicated to our first grandson, T.J. It's my hope that when his generation enters the workforce, the United States will be the world leader in innovation, manufacturing, technology, and customer service because of long-term, employee-oriented business leadership.

To my wife and best friend, Tess, my sons, John and Tim, our daughter-in-law Brittany, my mother and father Fred and Betty Knight, my wife's parents Lloyd and Connie Gates and their children and families, my brother and sister Tom Knight and Susan McCoy, and all our friends and family who have helped us create fulfilling lives in this great country.

I would also like to dedicate this book to the nurses, doctors, staff, and fellow volunteers at Riley Hospital who work to provide continually improving care for extremely ill children.

My final dedication is to Carl Para III who I met while volunteering at Riley. Although Carl passed away shortly after his 16th birthday he demonstrated amazing courage. Like many of the children at the hospital, Carl never complained and continually thought of others before himself. Business leaders today can learn from Carl's selflessness and courage.

Contents

1. Introduction: The Employee Induction Motor 1
2. We Got Lucky and then I Learned About Other Organizational Cultures 5

The Employee Induction Motor

3. Employees and Systems – The Basics 15
4. One Team with Structure and Flexibility 19
5. No Such Thing as Too Much Input. 23
6. Rewards, Recognition, and Honest Feedback 33
7. Creating Ecstatic Customers Takes a Great Organization. 37
8. Vendors, Regulators, and Outside Influences 51
9. Four Unwavering Principles All Employees Know. 57
10. You Can't Fake It!. 65
11. The Complete Employee Induction Motor 69

Employee Effectiveness Systems

12. Employee Induction Motor Training and Systems 73
13. Hiring and Integrating New Employees 77
14. Improvement, Communication, and Recognition Committees. 89
15. Input and Honest Discussion Improves Almost Every Issue. 93
16. Employee Recognition Systems. 99
17. Financial Rewards and Compensation 103
18. Employee Measurement Tools 107
19. Promotions 109
20. Honest Feedback and Performance Appraisals. 115
21. Nonperforming Employees 121

American Business in a Global Economy

22. What Has Changed in the United States? 129
23. What Has Changed in Today's Global Economy? 143
24. What Has Not Changed? 147
25. Traditional Leadership 153
26. Restructuring to Restructure Leadership 159
27. Engaged and Effective Employees - Not Zombies 171
28. Effective Leaders Are Humble Team Players -Not Royalty 177

29. Summary 185

Preface

This book is based on my thirty years of experience working with many organizations as an employee and a consultant. I am sure I am not the only American concerned as our manufacturing base continues to rapidly shrink at the same time trade deficits and government deficits are both approaching one trillion dollars per year. It is very difficult to pinpoint the cause and effect for the infinite number of variables that continually impact specific economies, and many feel the problem is that our wages are too high and we are too regulated. This argument does not explain how companies like Honda, Toyota, BMW, and their suppliers manufacture globally competitive products in hundreds of United States facilities. It also does not explain why countries like Germany employ twice the percentage of workers in manufacturing while confronting high employee and energy costs, as well as a very strict regulatory environment.

Our problem may be much simpler. Maybe our business leadership has gravitated towards making as much money in the very short-term as possible. This type of leadership does not allow the time or flexibility to gain employee input and buy-in. In this environment employees become frustrated and burned out and our ability to compete in a global market deteriorates.

This book is written in three major segments, the first segment titled *The Employee Induction Motor* (Chapters 3-11) discusses a business leadership model that fits on one page or one poster that has repeatedly proven to generate enthusiasm and buy-in from employees, customers, vendors, regulators, environmentalists, and investors. The model is based on employee input being the catalyst for continual improvement versus top-down short-term decisions.

The Employee Induction Motor can be customized for almost any business.

The second segment titled *Employee Effectiveness Systems* (Chapters 12-21) offers specific ideas to reinforce employee oriented leadership to excel long-term. This segment includes a chapter on how to interview to better assure strong employees are brought into and integrated into your organization. Hopefully there will be many ideas leaders can take from this section.

The final segment titled *American Business in a Global Economy* (Chapters 22-28) is really designed to be food for thought. This segment discusses what has and has not changed in a global economy. It also addresses possible reasons why the United States is losing manufacturing jobs. These loses may be more tied to this short-term trend in business leadership that has increased frustration for employees in many American industries. This final segment also includes some thoughts on changes in leadership styles, effective and engaged employees versus burned out employees, and the need for leaders to be humble and team oriented.

As anyone involved with leadership realizes leadership is not an exact science. I wrote this book based on the tremendous success I experienced using the simple leadership model called the Employee Induction Motor. This is a model we somewhat lucked into while turning around a national environmental business in the face of a severe industry recession. Our business was highly regulated and required long-term strategies and commitments because it took two to ten years to make even minor modifications to our operating permits. I have since found that this model works to help almost any business excel in a very competitive global environment.

The examples I use in this book are based on my experiences but are not meant to be an actual specific recounting of events for any of the fine organizations I had the privilege of working for as a consultant or an employee. I also am aware I do not have all of the answers. Even though I know these are great principles to follow, I

Preface

have on occasion not adhered to my own advice and found myself being a less than effective leader. The goal of this book is to provoke some thought and to present a one page simple leadership model that can be easily understood by all employees to help organizations excel. I hope you enjoy this book and come away with some ideas on how to strive to continually be a more effective business leader.

Bruce J. Knight

Chapter 1

Introduction: The Employee Induction Motor

Nearly 200 years ago, Michael Faraday discovered how invisible electric energy can be turned into motion - Faraday's law of induction. The idea is to use opposite forces that push and pull in perfect harmony to create smoothly running motors capable of generating almost any level of speed and torque. The simple design of electric motors means that they are very durable and efficient. Amazingly, today's electric motors not only drive the vehicle forward, but they can also actually generate electricity to recharge their batteries while traveling downhill or braking.

Because of their dependability and simple construction, electric motors were actually the first choice of some automobile manufacturers at the turn of the twentieth century. Over the next 100 years, piston engines that use explosions to create energy replaced electric motors as the preferred power source for vehicles. The problem with piston engines is that a large amount of energy is wasted in the up-and-down motion of the pistons and the heat from the continual explosions. Other problems include the limited supply of petroleum-derived fuel, the lack of a way to recapture energy, and the less-dependable nature of piston engines.

Twentieth-century leadership followed a similar path to that of the automobile engine. Leadership styles frequently became explosions generated by leaders who pushed their plans down on employees.

These dramatic, explosive decisions frequently changed direction like giant pistons. While certainly powerful, like combustion engines, this explosive style of leadership is inefficient and frequently burns out employees and systems.

Explosive leaders and coaches were sought after and admired in the United States. The charge was "Make a decision, even if it is wrong!" or "This is a dictatorship not a democracy!" The problem with explosive leadership is that it is not sustainable in a world market, where continual refinement of products, services, and systems is the key to success. Burned-out employees and high turnover are the wasted energy of explosive leadership, and just like piston motors, the explosions can become completely uncontrollable as the entire motor, or organization, melts down and grinds to a halt.

As we move into an age in which the world needs to develop sustainable and renewable options to reduce consumption and greenhouse gasses, the smooth, economical electric motor is becoming essential to keeping efficiency high in machines such as hybrid vehicles. Most renewable technologies such as hydrogen cells produce electricity, and they need efficient and powerful electric motors to create motion.

Many people do not think of electric motors as being particularly powerful and would probably be surprised to know that the drive wheels of mighty locomotives are 100 percent powered by electric motors. Even though the diesel engines onboard are huge, the torque required to start and stop the train would destroy them. Because electric motors are much more powerful and durable at any speed, the diesel engines on locomotives only operate generators to provide electricity, not to turn the train's wheels. Today, locomotives are by far the most efficient method of transporting freight over land, and fuel cells will no doubt replace the diesel engines in the future, allowing trains to become even more efficient and environmentally friendly.

Introduction: The Employee Induction Motor

As we move into the global market of the twenty-first century, leadership also needs to move away from explosive management styles. Employees must buy into strategies and decisions and believe there is a purpose beyond "How do we make money this quarter?" The Employee Induction Motor uses employee input and feedback to ensure almost every ounce of energy is focused toward continuous refinement instead of explosive changes in direction.

Chapter 2
We Got Lucky and then I Learned About Other Organizational Cultures

The concepts of the Employee Induction Motor were originally developed during the turnaround of a struggling nationwide environmental business. Part of a $1 billion chemical distribution company, our environmental business was only $10 million of the total revenue. At that time, we were part of one of the largest chemical distributor in the United States. In order to offer customers an outlet to dispose of spent chemicals the environmental business unit was started to collect drums of chemical waste. Initially my position was a staff position and I had only four people working for me, each responsible for assisting fifteen to twenty of the seventy chemical distribution branch locations with their chemical waste collection. A branch manager oversaw each location, and each branch was responsible for a specific area of the country. Customer service, sales, drivers, and warehouse all worked for the chemical distribution branch manager. The primary job for a branch manager was to sell industrial chemicals, although he was also asked to sell and manage the incredibly complex chemical waste program I was now assigned to oversee. This was a difficult assignment because the collection of chemical waste generally represented less than two percent of the branch's revenues.

I had been a branch manager in the chemical distribution company for six years before accepting the position to run the environmental business. I knew the branch manager job was a very busy, competitive job, and the tiny amount of chemical waste collected was a distraction for most of the branch managers. Most of the drums of waste collected contained pretty much the same chemicals found in consumer products such as spray paints, solvents, and oven cleaners - chemicals that might be stored under your sink or in your garage. At home you may be able to throw these liquids in the trash, but in an industrial setting they are classified as hazardous waste, and there are severe fines for improper disposal. It was not uncommon, at that time, to charge $500 per drum for collection and processing at an incinerator or recycling facility. Our environmental business did not own processing facilities; we simply collected the drums and shipped them to companies that charged us for recycling or destroying the waste. Even though we did not own processing facilities, our business required a substantial amount of long-term strategic thinking because modifications to the permits needed to run our business required two to ten years of close work with state agencies to finalize even the smallest changes. Our facilities were also subjected to intense inspection by state and federal agencies to assure compliance to extensive and complex regulations, with some locations being inspected on a weekly basis.

When I took over the environmental business the chemical waste industry was growing at an unbelievable rate of over 20 percent per year, and most of our competitors were making huge profits. Unfortunately, our business was heading in the opposite direction. Our tiny environmental business was in shambles. We were experiencing declining sales, zero profitability, poor morale, and worst of all, notices of serious violations from government inspectors were streaming in at the rate of nearly one every week.

Using input from our handful of employees, we developed a new leadership model that allowed us to turn the business around. I really believe the circumstances were just right for us to luck into the concepts behind the Employee Induction Motor. Because the most immediate and serious problem was to eliminate the barrage of violations, our number one assignment was to *do the right thing* at all times in terms of compliance, safety, and community awareness. Because the environmental industry was very strong, the assumption was that no matter what we did to fix the compliance issue, we would still be okay on the financial side. Despite the strong business environment I told my boss, "We will fix the compliance problem, but I am not sure if we will make a lot of money."

Only a year or so after I took over the business, industry growth dropped very quickly from 20 percent per year to nearly zero percent because manufacturers were tired of paying $500 a drum to get rid of waste products and therefore began to adjust their processes to eliminate and minimize waste. When industry growth was 20 percent, companies that processed waste were encouraged to build new incinerators and processing facilities across the country. Almost overnight the industry experienced a massive supply and demand imbalance, with far too much processing capacity for the reduced volume of chemical waste being generated. In response, average industry prices to process a drum of waste dropped by 50 percent or more.

Nobody expected the hazardous waste disposal industry would fall into this very steep recession. When this occurred, our competitors began to cut back and restructure at a frantic pace. Employee morale fell in our competitors' organizations, causing customer service to suffer, and their financial position worsened. For us it was exactly the opposite. We stayed focused on our four principles: 1) do the right thing, 2) keep our employees happy and effective, 3) make our customers ecstatic, and 4) ensure a strong financial return. I am still amazed at how good people feel about working for an organization that is truly committed to doing the right thing. These four principles, in this order, became our unwavering doctrine that we repeated at the beginning of each meeting. By working together as one team and by utilizing the four unwavering principles, our environmental business unit skyrocketed, and our return on investment jumped from zero to over 40 percent.

By the time the rest of the industry collapsed, we had created a completely separate and focused business unit within the chemical distribution company. Soon we were operating out of ten facilities across the country and employed our own sales, customer service, and driver/warehouseman personnel who were completely dedicated to collecting chemical waste. We now employed a little more than 100 people, and all of us could not wait to get to work each day. Even though we were spread across the country, we were one work family; the work seemed easy, and we enjoyed terrific success.

Most of the chemical waste processing companies began to experience severe financial hardships, including bankruptcy, but by using our new Employee Induction Motor leadership model during this period, our business flourished. Volumes increased by 800 percent and revenues increased from $10 million to $40 million. Operating profit increased to $4 million, and because we had no investment in inventory and little investment in property, our return on investment was aver 40 percent. Most importantly, notices of violations dropped from nearly fifty a year to zero. The amazing aspect was that it all seemed so easy. While our competitors were continually cutting back and restructuring, we focused on utilizing honest, open discussions to gain input from all our employees, so that we could provide the best customer service in the industry. We were also very unselfish about recognizing and rewarding employees. I still believe that slow economic times present opportunities for many companies to capitalize on the cutbacks made by their competitors.

Results for Our Nationwide Chemical Waste Business using the *Employee Induction Motor*

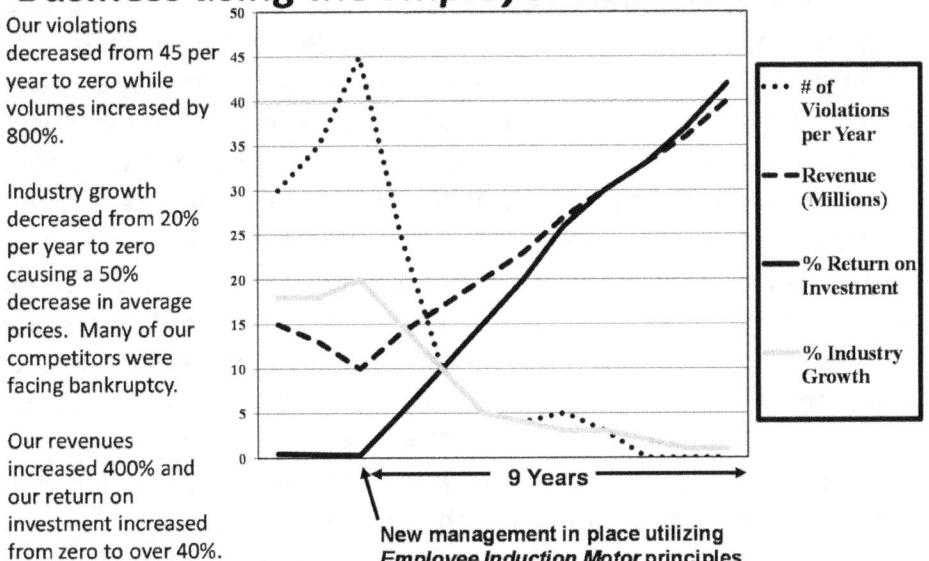

Our violations decreased from 45 per year to zero while volumes increased by 800%.

Industry growth decreased from 20% per year to zero causing a 50% decrease in average prices. Many of our competitors were facing bankruptcy.

Our revenues increased 400% and our return on investment increased from zero to over 40%.

New management in place utilizing *Employee Induction Motor* principles.

I Learned It Can Be Difficult to Change an Organization's Culture

Our success prompted several larger environmental companies to offer me senior manager positions. I turned down several offers (mostly because I wanted to keep our family in the Midwest) before I decided to accept a senior management position at a larger environmental company, where my new assignment was to help grow sales, profits, and expand business nationwide. This new environmental company seemed to have all the necessary assets for success, but its performance had been lackluster since the industry downturn. The owners were not happy with the continued weak performance in their environmental company. Every few years the owners would bring in a new senior executive to help reinvigorate the company. The owners pushed the new leaders to make sweeping and dramatic changes to take the company in a new direction. I was the third attempt since the performance stagnated and based on the success I had with my former employer, I was sure I could help my new company turn the corner. Unfortunately, I found out it was not as easy as I had thought.

When I arrived I found an organization that was completely burned out due to the continual changes in leaders and directions. In my new assignment as vice president of sales, I was thought of as "the sales guy," and I was pretty much asked to "do my sales thing." Although we assembled a strong national sales team, I knew we needed to do more. I explained that the key to my prior success was that we developed an organizational structure that utilized honest input and discussion from all employees to provide outstanding customer service resulting in strong overall performance. We were also unselfish in recognizing and rewarding contributors. We encouraged these ideals through four unwavering principles that every employee clearly understood. I led the implementation of a similar program at my new employer, and after presenting the program to all 1,000 employees, internal surveys showed that 94 percent to 99 percent of employees were very positive about the new program. Unfortunately employees and even management were so burned out the program faded away.

As part of the program we assembled improvement teams made up of employees from many disciplines to provide recommendations to the rest of the senior management team. Our team members recommended that we provide services that would make us more efficient and distinguish us from our competition - services like calling and e-mailing customers in advance of waste collections in a specific geography and installing lift gates in every truck. It was these types of benefits that allowed us to excel at my former employer. We explained that these services actually saved money and improved profits because of the increased efficiency of the trucking operation and increased sales from satisfied customers. By calling all customers in an area before collection and having lift gates on all trucks, the need to make repeat trips with partially full trucks was dramatically reduced. Waste from all customers in a given area was picked up on one trip - no one was forgotten, and drums of waste could be picked up even if customers did not have access to a loading dock. The additional benefit was that these features gave our sales force powerful and real benefits to differentiate themselves from most of the competition. Customers were required by law to ship their chemical waste every ninety days, and there were stiff penalties for noncompliance. By putting customers on a schedule, calling ahead of our trucks, and having the equipment to get the job done, we could take a huge burden off of the customer. However, in spite of enthusiasm from members of the improvement teams there was little support from senior management to proceed forward on these initiatives.

After only a few years a new president was brought in and everything I tried to implement was again restructured and in a few more years he left and another restructuring cycle began. In order to cut costs under the latest plan only fifteen people were assigned to answer calls from customers to place orders for chemical waste to be shipped out of their facility. An internal survey conducted during working hours from 8:00 a.m. to 5:00 p.m. confirmed that 50 percent of the time customers received voice mail when they called customer service personnel. Keep in mind that many of these customers were running up against the ninety-day federal limit on storing hazardous wastes. Needless to say, customers in a hurry to ship waste out were not pleased to call during business hours only to be asked to leave a voice mail and then hope someone calls back to arrange shipment of their waste within the required time frame. I saw this as a fundamental flaw and highly recommended increasing the number of personnel assigned to answer incoming phone calls however, even managers seemed to burned out to care. Having previously managed an organization designed to create ecstatic customers, it was hard for me to continue working for a company who did not answer the phone when customers called to place an order. The company's performance remained lackluster and I decided to move on.

After eight years, I departed on good terms and started my own consulting business. I was reinvigorated over the next few years when I was able to assist two new companies to achieve record success utilizing the leadership concepts presented in the Employee Induction Motor. For the purposes of this book I will call these companies Lamp Recyclers and Resin Recyclers.

One of the reasons I wrote this book was because I remember how easy everything was at the environmental business we had created within the chemical distribution company and how difficult everything seemed when I accepted a job at a different environmental company. The second environmental company I worked for employed ten times more people although its revenues were only three times more. In fairness, this company did offer some more labor-intensive services; however, the difference in headcount and performance between the two organizations was substantial, as the following chart illustrates:

Comparison of different organizations

	Organization A	Organization B
Revenue	$40 million	$120 million
Return on Investement	35-45%	Below 5%
Total Employees	100	1000
Corporate Personnel	6	60
Sales Personnel	30	30
Customer Service Personnel	30	15
Notices of Violations	Zero for prior three years	Some Violations

Even more frustrating than the inefficiency was the work environment - most people were not very happy. The continual changes created an environment where there was no sense of being part of a team. In fact, employees who had been employed for many years liked to say that new employees were not *company people* (whatever that meant).

Many employees reminded me of zombies. These employees pretty much came to work every day, complained to each other, sat in their office or cubicle, and exchanged e-mails until it was time to go home. Instead of talking to each other, employees had a tendency to keep adding on to the same e-mail, until the e-mail strings would extend twenty or thirty e-mails long. At the end of the day, I am not sure anyone felt they accomplished much. My departure was prompted when I realized that I was becoming a zombie employee, also. At this point I was as much a part of the problem as anyone else in the organization. Zombie employees are highly contagious.

The good news is that this organization finally settled on a humble president who utilized employee input to gradually evolve in place of constant drastic restructuring. Many years have passed, and as I understand this company is now performing at a much higher level under new leadership.

"Zombie" employees

- Do not believe their ideas count
- Do not feel they will be fairly recognized or rewarded
- Dislike their job and simply put in their time
- At the end of the day contribute little to the organization

These type of employees are so prevalent a new genre of comedy has developed around them – "The Office," "Dilbert," "Office Space."

Sadly however, when I talk to friends who work for other organizations, they also complain about their jobs and the frustration of sitting in a cubicle e-mailing all day with little feeling of accomplishment. The zombie trend has become so prevalent in this country that it has spawned a new genre of comedy that includes the Dilbert comic strip, the movie *Office Space*, and the tremendously successful television show *The Office*. Scott Adams, the creator of Dilbert, has always received many of his ideas from fans who simply write in about their experiences at work. Adams recently updated his web site to allow visitors to actually write new comics themselves. Because of the new era of business leadership, Adams now has the easiest job in this country.

One of the repercussions of a high number of zombie employees is that the people who are actually effective at their jobs become overworked and increasingly frustrated. These higher performing employees frequently accept positions in different companies, increasing the percentage of zombie employees left behind.

Using the concepts presented in the Employee Induction Motor, Lamp Recyclers, Resin Recyclers and the environmental business we built within the chemical distribution company, all avoided a prevalence of the zombie syndrome. It was very clear that most employees were effective and enjoyed working for those organizations. Growth in these organizations was through continued refinement, not drastic reorganizations, as they found ways to utilize employee input and innovation so that employees remained motivated to outperform the competition in heavily regulated and very competitive industries.

The Employee Induction Motor

Chapter 3
The Basics - Employees and Systems

The idea of the Employee Induction Motor is to boil business down to a simple visual diagram of basic components that everyone can believe in and understand. Similar to the way efficient and smooth running electric motors are helping to improve mechanical efficiencies, the Employee Induction Motor is a smooth running and efficient leadership model designed to help with organizational efficiencies.

The two basic components for the Employee Induction Motor are employees and systems. These are really the only two parts to any business organization. The definition of systems includes anything that can be adjusted, modified, or changed besides the employees themselves, including facilities, operations, computers, equipment, and procedures. It is the relationship between employees and systems that creates an exceptional organization.

There are only two components in every business organization.

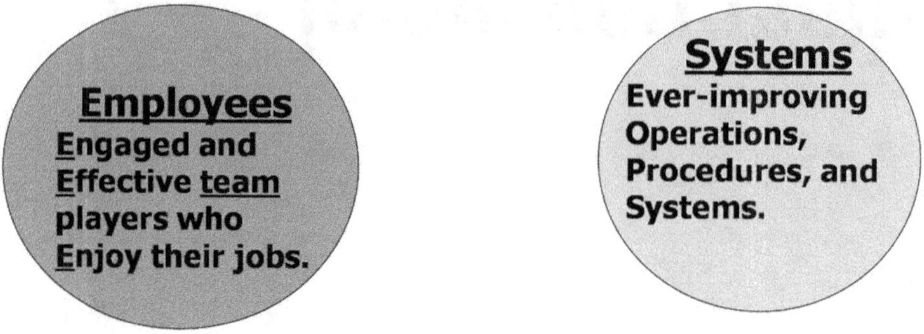

Employees
Engaged and
Effective **team**
players who
Enjoy their jobs.

Systems
Ever-improving
Operations,
Procedures, and
Systems.

The following diagram illustrates the impact of the overall effectiveness of employees and systems on an organization.

Impact of employees and systems on an organization

Employees ↑	**Mediocre Organization** Engaged, effective, and motivated employees working as one team can overcome many systems deficiencies, however they cannot overcome a lack of investment in sophisticated robotics and assembly equipment required for manufacturing.	**Exceptional Organization** Engaged, effective, and motivated employees working as one team coupled with effective and ever-improving systems.
	Failing Organization Zombie employees, high employee turnover, little teamwork, and poor systems.	**Poor Organization** Effective systems cannot overcome zombie employees, high employee turnover, and little teamwork. Systems will also deteriorate over time.

Systems →

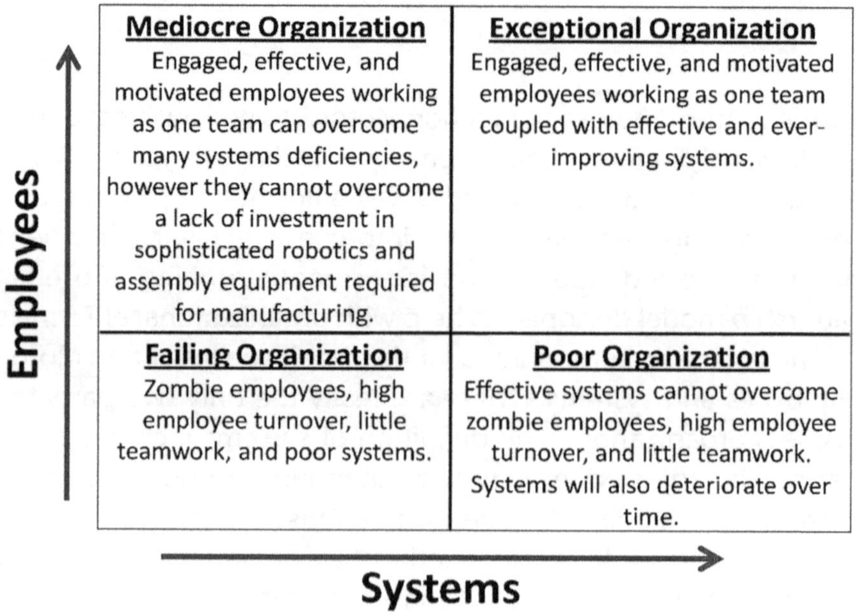

Contrary to what many business leaders believe, failing organizations are the result of poor systems and zombie employees, not a result of too much competition or reduced demand for products and services offered. The proof of this conclusion is easy to find. Many companies that have been in existence for more than a few decades no longer produce the products and services they originally offered. When I was in the chemical business, Pfizer was basically synonymous with the production of citric acid. Pfizer developed the process to produce citric acid in the 1800's and they were the world's largest producer for a century (Pfizer, 2009). Because citric acid later became a commodity product, and Pfizer saw themselves as a specialty chemical producer, Pfizer sold their citric acid business. In the chemical industry this seemed like the equivalent of Kleenex deciding not to sell tissues any longer, but in actuality, changes like this happen all the time. There are many European companies that have been in business for hundreds of years. I am sure these companies are not all still offering the same products and services they originally sold in the 1700's. It is the success of their employees and systems that have allowed them to succeed by continuing to refine their product and service offerings to meet customer's ever changing demands.

It is the responsibility of business leaders to create an environment where employees utilize honest communication to continually improve systems to produce products and services that meet buyers needs better than their competition. If an organization's products and services are no longer needed, or they are not as good as the competition, it is up to employees to identify and implement required changes to create better products and services.

As you can see by the chart, even good systems cannot overcome zombie employees, and although strong employees can overcome poor systems in many service industries, it is impossible to overcome weak systems in industries like manufacturing that requires a large investment in capital equipment to maintain state of the art systems.

Chapter 4
One Team with Structure and Flexibility

It is a top priority for business leaders to build a unified team dedicated to ensuring the organization has the best systems and employees in place to serve customers better than their competition. It cannot be just about the leaders; when the team suffers, everyone suffers, and when the team wins, everyone wins. Leaders need to treat everyone fairly and abide by the same rules as everyone else. Employees in successful organizations experience the three E's, they are *Engaged*, *Effective*, and consequently they *Enjoy* their jobs. Employees are represented as one circle in the Employee Induction Motor because all employees from the CEO to a newly hired intern need to act as one unified team to become an exceptional organization.

Employees are represented in one tight circle because:

In order to be successful organizations need to operate as <u>one team</u> of <u>Engaged</u> and <u>Effective</u> Employees who <u>Enjoy</u> what they do for a living...

<u>**Employees**</u>
<u>E</u>ngaged and
<u>E</u>ffective <u>team</u>
players who
<u>E</u>njoy their jobs.

Representing employees as one team does not mean that there is not structure required within an organization. This is where systems come into play. As we will discuss in following chapters, ever-improving systems need to be in place to service customers, and interface with vendors, regulators, the community, and the environment. To enjoy long-term success, organizations also need ever-improving systems that ensure employees are fairly hired, compensated, promoted, rewarded, recognized, measured, and given honest feedback. Systems must be in place to provide hierarchy, job descriptions, compensation, and appraisals. From what I have witnessed, the recent trend toward short-sighted continual restructuring has negatively affected many organizations by either creating a very inflexible and outdated structure, or by having little structure at all. Often it seems that small- and medium-sized businesses have few systems in place to promote employee input and effectiveness, and larger organizations have inflexible systems that inhibit employee input and involvement.

To operate as one team, different departments and areas need to work together without allowing egos to become involved. Human resources should not be some far-off staff position that only gets involved when someone is fired, hired, or disciplined. The same is true of compliance, safety, information technology, sales, accounting, and other facets. With the Employee Induction Motor model, there is really no such thing as a staff position in the traditional sense - everyone is a key member of the team. Organizational hierarchies really do need to be more horizontal and avoid excessive layers of leadership.

Resin Recyclers subscribed to the Employee Induction Motor model and I worked with them to develop a company Improvement, Communication, and Recognition (ICR) team that consisted of managers from every major department, including sales, customer service, IT, compliance, safety, accounting, and human resources. Even though I worked for Resin Recyclers as a consultant, I also attended all of the ICR team meetings. Meetings were held every two weeks and lasted about an hour and a half. Notes were kept, and there was a crisp agenda for every meeting. Anything that could not be resolved in the meeting was assigned to a team of a few people who would consider the issue and report back to the committee at the next meeting. Members of this group did not possess big egos, honestly presented their views, listened to everyone, and did not try to dominate the conversation. It was agreed early on that these would be the requirements for anyone who joined the committee. The lasting results this committee generated within the organization were amazing. This was a national $60 million company with over 300 employees, and this one committee helped the organization become one of the most successful in its industry.

In a stark contrast another company I worked with was all over the place in terms of improvement committees. When I first arrived, the company was being led by a team of three executives who rarely met and typically gave different messages. During one of their restructuring trends, a new senior leader was brought in who decided to form improvement committees. He created seven different improvement committees that operated independently. Each committee had ten members, and they were instructed to meet in person at least once a month for a full day. Once a quarter, these committees would put on skits for all the managers during a two-day meeting. Preparation for these skits might take several days, and the cost for these committees, including travel, salaries, and benefits, was approximately $1 million per year for a company that was struggling to make $4 million in profit. I am convinced that the one and a half hour meetings at Resin Recyclers attended by conference call and in person were far more productive than the man all day improvement committee meetings.

Chapter 5
No Such Thing as Too Much Input

I recently read a quote from Admiral Michael Glenn "Mike" Mullen, USN, (2009) who is the seventeenth chairman of the Joint Chiefs of Staff. Admiral Mullen said he is driven by a piece of advice he received in a letter when he became an admiral. Mullen says, "The line that I remember the most from all those letters was 'Congratulations, just remember one thing: from now on you will always eat well - and you'll never hear the truth again.' And that stuck with me." Admiral Mullen frequently visits the front lines and talks with troops on the ground. He tells troops, "You see it in a way that I can't. So I need help from you in seeing what's really going on."

Repowering American Industry!

Mike Mullen

**Joint Chief of Staff Chairman U.S. Military
Continually visits front line personnel to gain their input.**

He is driven by advice he received in a letter when he was promoted to Admiral.

"The line that I remember most was 'Congratulations – just remember one thing: from now on you will always eat well and <u>you will never hear the truth again.</u>' And that stuck with me."

I have spent many years at corporate headquarters that are full of executives who eat well and never hear the truth. Many of the problems associated with the environmental business unit I took over were created because leaders did not want to hear the truth. Leadership decided that the drums of chemical waste should be sold, collected, and managed by the same employees who delivered the virgin chemicals; after all, they were basically the same products. Unfortunately, the regulatory requirements, knowledge and expertise required to handle virgin and waste products were completely different. Because leadership did not listen to employees well enough to understand this, the business struggled.

While I was running the environmental business unit, one of the presidents at the chemical distribution company named Doug created the Call Doug Line. Memos went out telling employees they could leave a message for Doug on any subject and Doug would reply. When I was forced to severely demote one of my subordinates because of one poor presentation, one of his former employees left a message for Doug that management had wrongly demoted a great manager. Instead of addressing the comments, I was reprimanded because this topic was off-limits for the Call Doug Line, and our employee should have somehow known this. Clearly Doug did not seem interested in hearing the truth.

Many leaders' egos will not allow them to hear the truth. The president and owner of one company for which I consulted told me that its biggest advantage over the competition was a new computer program that interacted directly with customers. He went on and on about how this was a huge advantage over their competition. I worked with the company for only a few weeks when I realized that only a handful of their 1,000 customers were using this new system. Everyone was afraid to tell the president that only a few customers were using the new system, and the president was content to not know the truth.

Many people in leadership roles do not like honest input because it may go against their ideas, and they feel it challenges their leadership. Worse, part of our culture tends to think people who listen to too much input are not strong leaders because they do not make quick, independent decisions or stick to their course of action. I have actually been told by supporters of failed leaders, "You have to give him credit. At least he stuck to his guns!" To me this is similar to giving credit to a school bus driver who did not turn the wheel when the bus was headed off a cliff.

Utilizing honest input from employees is an area where Japanese management has excelled. The Japanese learned that it is critical to gain as much input as possible, particularly when manufacturing products. Employees at Japanese auto manufacturing companies were encouraged to stop the assembly line if they identified an ongoing problem. The problem was then fixed, so that it did not occur again. This type of thinking allowed the Japanese to build higher-quality automobiles. At the same time the Japanese were allowing workers to stop the assembly line, American workers were fired if they stopped the assembly line, even if every automobile was passing through with obvious and serious defects (Olsen & Cabadas, 2002). The idea was to assemble cars and not to be bothered with the truth about the car's actual quality. When I was growing up I remember that many people liked to criticize the Japanese by remarking that the Japanese never invent everything - they just keep improving on pre-existing ideas. My answer to this complaint is "Duh, since when is there a law against improvement?" Few great and totally new inventions come along; the key to success is continually improving existing products and services.

One problem with not listening to input is very obvious. Everyone dislikes know-it-alls, and yet leaders who do not listen to input and "stick to their guns" are positioning themselves as omniscient know-it-alls that no one really respects. The benefit of listening to as much input as possible is that it encourages engaged employees. People want their opinion to be heard. Leaders obviously cannot change the direction of the organization based on every suggestion, but leaders can listen to and consider every suggestion.

Leadership at one company I worked with seemed to answer almost every suggestion for improvement with, "Let me tell you why that won't work," or "We tried that before, and it did not work." It does not take long before people start becoming zombies and quit offering any ideas for improvement. It takes discipline for leaders to eliminate negative responses to employee's ideas for improvement.

Another problem with not listening to enough input is that managers can instead adopt a "Superman" leadership model where the manager tries to do it all themselves and does not ask much from anyone else. This may be successful for a while, but eventually mangers either wear out, or the business stops growing because there is always a limit to what one person can accomplish.

Effective leaders need to eliminate negative responses to input such as:
- Let me tell you why that won't work.
- We tried that before and it did not work.
- You are just making excuses.
- Let me tell you why we do it that way.

Replace those comments with:
- Tell me more.
- Thank you for your input, and please keep coming to me with ideas.
- We may not be able to do anything immediately, but we will continue to listen to your ideas to help us become a better organization.

To compete in the new global market, products, services, and systems need to be continually refined. The only way to accomplish this is for leaders to foster engaged employees and ask for and utilize a tremendous amount of employee input, whether it is positive and negative. To accomplish this, effective leaders need to keep their egos in check, and remember what I call the leadership paradox - If a leader thinks they are a great leader, they are almost certainly not a great leader. All leaders have room to improve, however big egos almost always get in the way of being a good listener and learner.

As a leader it is easy to say you will listen to employee input while it is much harder to actually listen to input on a regular basis. I recall one incident when I volunteered to design a new company brochure. I brought an initial draft to a middle manager I respected and asked her what she thought. She said, "You want my honest opinion?" I said, "Of course." Her response was, "Well, I think it sucks!" I can tell you that I was pretty ticked off at her comment because I had already put a week or so into the draft and had run it by many employees. Instead of being defensive, I took a breath and asked her why she felt that way. She said it was much too wordy and I used her advice to make it a much more useful document.

I am sure many leaders are telling themselves that they do listen to input and recognize their employees. I am also sure many employees are thinking, "I wish my boss or senior management would listen to me and recognize me or my department." As a leader, you cannot ever listen to enough input or give enough recognition because employees crave both. Above all else, it is these two currents that power great organizations. Employees want to be happy and effective in their work, and yet many employees dread going to work. Having their input heard and being fairly recognized and rewarded keeps employee morale high. It is these currents that power the Employee Induction Motor. These currents create forward motion and power in any organization.

When I started consulting I decided to begin by meeting individually with ten or so employees in an organization. I asked each person two questions: "If this was your company what would you do?" and "What could be done to help you do your job better?" In almost every case, in spite of senior managers talking about the openness of their company, employees said "I know what the problem is, but I am not going to be the one to point it out." Employees also almost always point out the same areas for improvement. In a couple of hours speaking with a handful of employees from different departments, it usually becomes clear where many of the major problems are within an organization. That is the easy part. The hard part is honestly sharing these very real issues with management because, more times than not, management struggles with accepting honest input. Even well-run companies like Resin Recyclers can have trouble listening to real input. Almost every salesperson at Resin Recyclers complained about the auto reimbursement plan because the plan rewarded sales personnel who did not travel and penalized those who worked the hardest. A new plan was proposed that did not cost much more and actually offered better liability protection for the company. I brought this up to the president, and he snapped, "We are not ever changing our auto compensation plan!" Talk about rejecting employee input!

Leaders must seek out the truth and encourage all employees to provide and listen to honest input.

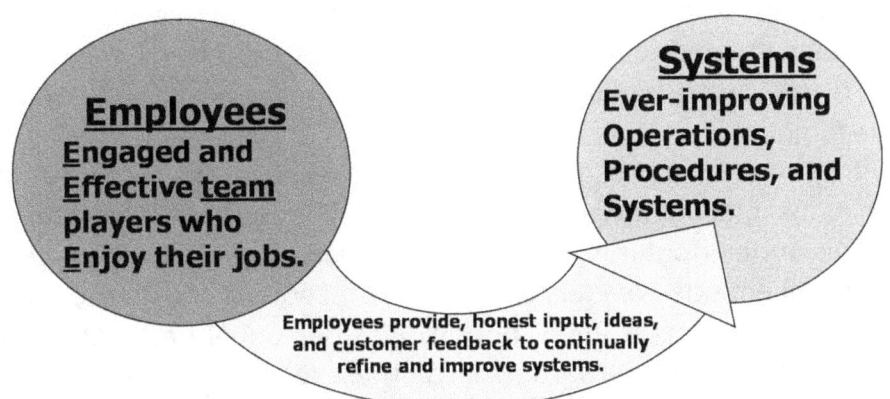

All employees (including leaders) must be Engaged, Effective, Team players who Enjoy their job.

The arching arrow depicted above in the Employee Induction Motor illustrates how employees must be constantly encouraged to provide honest feedback to continually improve systems. In short, this means that all employees must feel comfortable at times telling the emperors (company leaders) that they have no clothes. I have personally witnessed relatively few organizations where employees are this comfortable due to their fear of offending the egos of their leadership. This is an area where Jeff Blashill, the extremely successful head coach of the Indianapolis Ice hockey team excels. When he finishes a meeting he tells attendees he does not want anything left on the table. If you have something to say, say it. This coach clearly wants to hear the truth.

I have also noticed that most companies have very few systems in place to encourage input from employees. These companies are missing out on the type of feedback that continually improves products, services, and overall performance while also keeping employees motivated and engaged.

Historically, top-down management has frequently been encouraged and admired. Gathering input and making logical decisions to continually refine systems is not perceived as dynamic and glamorous as is making sweeping changes to head in an entirely new direction.

Input needs to be gathered from all levels of an organization. Traditional management tends to treat the line worker like a machine, and his or her input is not requested or heard. I have also witnessed technically-minded leaders who did not recognize or listen to input from sales personnel, even though sales personnel frequently best understand a customer's true needs. These leaders tend to see sales people as employees who want to cave to the customer's demands and are only making excuses for why they cannot make the sale.

In his book *Frames of Mind* (1993), psychologist Howard Gardner says that there are seven distinct kinds of intelligence. For example, people who gravitate to jobs where they work more with their hands (like a line worker) are better at spatial or body-kinesthetic intelligence, which allows them to think three dimensionally more easily and have better hand-eye coordination. People with strong interpersonal intelligence frequently gravitate toward and do well in sales positions. While some people are not strong in traditional scholastic skills, they may bring a new perspective to a problem and be able to think through issues with which those with scholastic intelligence may struggle.

Gardner's theory of different types of intelligence makes it clear that everyone offers unique insights or types of intelligence, and it is important to recognize everyone in an organization when gathering input. When I have made sales calls on Honda the opinion of every member of their supplier evaluation committee, including maintenance and assembly line workers was valued. In calling on many hundreds of American companies I did not ever encounter these types of employees on a supplier evaluation committee. Instead, the usual practice was for a purchasing agent to pressure suppliers to buy the cheapest product available, even if it caused major problems for the actual users.

Unfortunately from an educational and employee-promotion perspective, the United States is trending toward a culture that focuses primarily on what Gardner calls linguistic and logical-mathematical intelligence - what I refer to as scholastic intelligence. It's assumed that a person who does not read well or solve math problems utilizing traditional methods is not intelligent, and there is little need to gather their input. This is now being reinforced in our school systems with standardized testing that only tests students for scholastic intelligence. The fact that we do not perceive any need to test, recognize, or gain input from people with strong spatial or body-kinesthetic intelligence may be another reason the United States is losing manufacturing jobs. We certainly need input from employees with strong educational backgrounds; however, we also need employees who work with their hands and understand how devices such as a lathe actually operate. Many of our greatest inventions came from people who worked with their hands.

In terms of education, I was a classic C/B student. I always found the classroom setting very restrictive, and I was a daydreamer. Instead of paying attention, I was frequently designing or building something in my mind. When push came to shove, I knew I could always cram enough in a short period of time to at least get a C. A hot rod I recently built with a friend of mine named Kenny is a good example of what can be accomplished utilizing hands-on intelligence. I did most of the design work and fabrication, and Kenny did most of the mechanical and electrical work. Like many mechanics, Kenny never even thought about pursuing higher education, but he is very intelligent when it comes to making a car run. While it takes teams of engineers at a car company many years to design a new car, Kenny and I built a pretty respectable vehicle in a year—and on a budget. I think we sometimes miss out on this kind of hands-on intelligence in our pursuit of scholastic intelligence.

I have a son who is dyslexic but intelligent in terms of kinesthetic intelligence. Early in grade school, he was given the Wechsler Intelligence Scale for Children test. He scored very high in spatial awareness and three-dimensional thinking but very low in coding, which is essentially reading. My son and a friend built a complex high horsepower four-wheel-drive pulling truck with over 700 horsepower that is very competitive in his class on a very reasonable budget. My son's truck is outperforming trucks costing three and four times more to build. It would be interesting to compare the cost and performance of a truck built by a team of engineers to compete in the same class. Clearly highly educated engineers are critical to industry and we could not design and build much without them, it is simply that they too can learn from those on the assembly line who work with their hands for a living.

When I began consulting for Resin Recyclers, I asked to speak with the "folks out back," as the company referred to the line workers. These were union employees responsible for processing grimy drums of waste paints, solvents, and other industrial chemicals. The president of the company said I was more than welcome to speak with them, but he doubted that they would be interested in responding to my questions. The president could not have been more wrong. These were the most energetic and excited group to discuss the Employee Induction Motor and they provided the most input for improvement. In general, they were very frustrated because their input was not heard and did not count. They also felt that leaders in the company took them for granted and did not recognize their contribution.

Gathering and considering input from all levels is a leadership skill that is not just for managers; all employees need to act as leaders, and seek out and listen to input from other employees. Innovation comes from employee input, and when you squelch their contributions with rapidly implementing reorganization and restructuring from the top, you are also diminishing innovation in our country.

Chapter 6
Rewards, Recognition, and Honest Feedback

When employees provide input and energy to improve an organization, there must be systems in place to ensure those employees are recognized and rewarded. I am certain that Admiral Mullen knows that when he mingles with and listens to input from front-line troops, he is giving them a powerful sign of recognition.

    The arrow at the top of the Employee Induction Motor illustrates the need for systems to provide rewards, recognition, and honest feedback to employees. The better a leader recognizes and addresses contributions from employees, the more effective the organization. Effective leaders must ensure fair systems are in place and utilized to reward, recognize, measure, hire, and promote employees. Although leaders in well run organizations should be providing far more positive feedback than negative, effective leaders must also ensure fair systems are in place and utilized to provide honest feedback for employee improvement and to address non-performing employees. Like all systems, these need to be continually improved and refined. If leaders are effectively doing all of this while also listening to and utilizing employee input, there should consequently be very little turnover within an organization. Minimal turnover is critically important to build exceptional organizations. If organizations are constantly hiring and firing, then they need to address their leadership skills and the systems they are utilizing, that are illustrated by the two arching arrows of the Employee Induction Motor. The middle section in this book is devoted to providing examples I have witnessed to work successfully to help ensure these systems are in effect and utilized.

Systems must also be continually refined to improve employee teamwork, effectiveness, and satisfaction

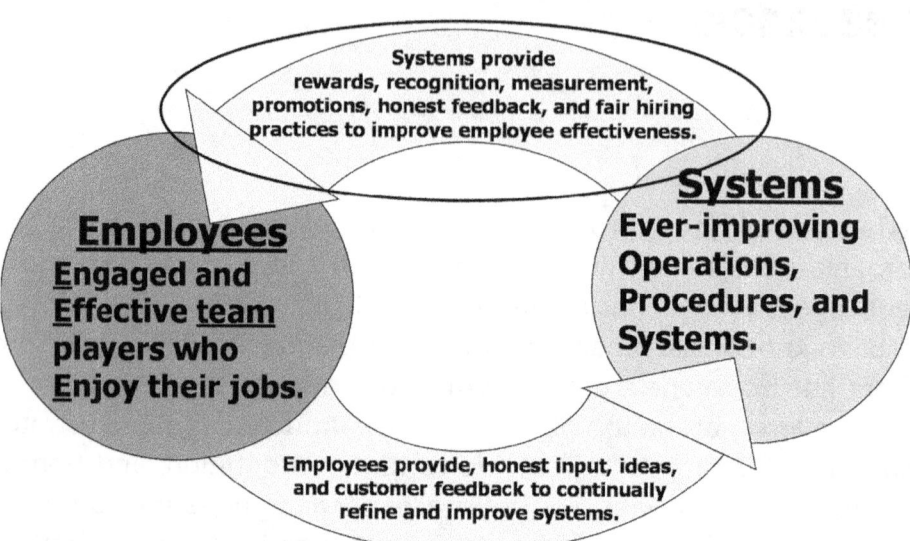

Of all of the areas covered by the top arrow in the Employee Induction Motor, recognition is probably the most important. While some employees may say recognition is not a big motivator, all employees crave recognition and I have known many good employees who have eventually quit jobs because of a lack of validation. This was first discovered in the well publicized Hawthorne experiments in the 1930's at the Hawthorne Works in Cicero, Illinois (Mayo, 1949). These studies introduced the idea that effectiveness improved when workers received humane treatment, personal attention, and a chance to feel wanted. Performance improved simply because workers received recognition in terms of attention.

The original intent of the experiments was to determine how lighting impacted workers. Instead the findings indicated that employees wanted to contribute and feel wanted, and productivity picked up simply because management was interested in what the workers were doing and accomplishing.

I worked for a company where the president seemed to consistently find reasons not to recognize employees. One of the improvement committees at this company recommended implementing a system to allow any employee to recognize another employee's contribution by simply filling out a form. The reward was to be a small blurb in the company newsletter and a signed certificate from the president, but senior managers, following the president's lead, were very upset at the idea of any form of recognition. Once the program started, the senior managers rejected almost every person employees wanted to recognize. One manager complained, "We cannot simply recognize everyone for doing their job!" It was no wonder this company was full of zombies.

It boggles my mind that there are leaders whose philosophy is that you cannot recognize people for simply doing their job. In my opinion leaders are not doing their job if they do not consistently recognize employees for doing theirs. This type of recognition does not cost the company a penny and is huge for employee morale. If anyone has coached little league they know how important it is to constantly tell the kids, "Good job!," "Nice work!," "Thanks for the extra effort!," "Way to go!," This type of positive reinforcement costs nothing, yet business leaders mostly only seem to point out what employees do wrong, or say little at all about employees' efforts.

I would strongly recommend that anyone reading this book go back into work tomorrow and try and give verbal recognition as many times as possible to subordinates or co-workers. Use the phrases: "Good job!," "Nice work!," "Thanks for the extra effort!," and be sincere. Recognize that people are trying to do their best. Believe in your fellow employees and you will be amazed at the results.

Chapter 7
Creating Ecstatic Customers Requires a Great Organization!

I started my career as a sales representative for a chemical distribution company immediately after graduating from college. The company had decided to hire sales representative trainees who had degrees in sales and marketing instead of chemistry. Management thought this would mean the sales staff would be driven to sell rather than spend time talking with chemists at customer locations. To some degree the plan worked. I felt I did not have much to fall back on and was driven to sell something. I attended a three-month training program that combined a crash course in basic chemistry with information about the company. After the program, we were assigned to one of the seventy facilities across the country.

I was ridiculously skinny and scared to death. My vision of a traveling salesperson was a guy in a plaid jacket passing out cigars and slapping people on the back. People talked about salespeople who were so slick that they could sell air conditioners to Eskimos. I did not feel that I was remotely like that person.

I was so green I think they sent me to one of the smaller locations in the Midwest, where I could do as little harm as possible. My new boss was only twenty-seven-years old. He was boyish in his enthusiasm, and he encouraged me to take it slow at first. I remember making my first call on a small prospect and providing him a written quote, with a competitive price. He told me my price was a little better and then asked, "So why should I buy from you?" In spite of all my training, I froze and could not think of a single thing to say.

In time, I realized how lucky I was to have such an enthusiastic manager supporting my sales efforts. I jokingly told people that if I could convince people to call Tom, he would sell them something. I began to realize that selling new customers and taking care of existing customers is really a team effort. In addition to Tom, our branch facility also employed two very competent customer service people named Carol and Peggy, as well as five dedicated and hard working driver/warehousemen who delivered chemicals to our customers.

Taking care of customers was about being sincere, understanding the customer's needs, and then trying to meet those needs. It was about doing what we said we were going to do, and often, it was about trying to make amends if we did not meet the customer's expectations. In most cases, everyone in our location interacted positively and developed very good relationships with our customers. Our customer service personnel and drivers frequently proved to be our best salespeople. I found it almost impossible to sell a customer a service we were not proficient at providing or a product the customer really did not need. Much to my relief, it was not at all about me wearing a plaid coat and selling air conditioners to Eskimos. I began to evaluate prospects and spend more time selling to accounts we could better service based on our product mix and geography. A list was distributed monthly that ranked the forty salespeople in our region. To my surprise, I eventually began to consistently lead the list in new accounts generated.

In my first assignment out of college, I once again found I was part of a work family. Granted, we still had problems on occasion, but overall we were a strong team, and that made it a lot easier for me to represent the company to existing and prospective customers. Shortly before I was transferred from this location my branch manager was promoted, and his replacement was much more of a dictator. Immediately after our new manager arrived, I was in his office when he was about to call our Chicago location to determine the availability of a product. As he picked up the phone, I asked him if he would mind also asking a question about another product for me. He slammed the phone down and very sternly said, "Don't you think you should call them yourself?!" It was very clear he considered himself a cut above everyone else because he was the manager. Working was nowhere near as much fun, and sales and profits began to slide for that location. Fortunately for me I was soon promoted away from this location.

Without a strong team-driven organization, there is no way to keep customers ecstatic in the long-term. I recently ate at a restaurant where the food and the service were fantastic. I was shocked to hear that they had only been open for three days. I asked the server how this was possible, and she replied that the ownership was dedicated to hiring the right people and making the customer's experience special. She said all employees went through significant training and by the time the restaurant opened, they had a great team in place to take care of customers. She told me that she had worked for many organizations that *said* employees were their most important asset, however this was the first organization that *meant it*.

This is a critical cultural issue within organizations. Leadership needs to "walk the talk". I was recently at a meeting of local environmental managers where a Toyota employee was enthusiastically presenting their team approach to improving systems to ensure problems do not reoccur. He was asked by an employee of an American car company how they incentivize employees to join and proactively participate on these improvement teams. His answer was also that Toyota says that employees are their number one *asset* and that they *mean it*. Employees join the committees not for money, but for recognition and a chance to contribute. The speaker said he has been a Toyota employee for 15 years and he has always felt very valued and recognized even though he started at the very bottom when he joined the company. He also added that the president of their forklift division, who is also on the Board of Directors for Toyota worldwide, sits in an open office and is on a fist name basis with all employees. The gentleman from the American car company almost seemed puzzled that anyone would join a committee simply for recognition and the chance to contribute.

I thought back to when I was an up and coming manager at the chemical distribution company when I was given the "privilege" to be a chauffeur for members of the company's board when they flew into town for a board meeting. My assignment was to pick them up as they arrived at a private airport in corporate jets. I assumed board members would be interested in chatting with their drivers/mid-level managers to get a feel for how things were going within the company. Instead these board members did not even speak with me. I specifically remember two of them casually chatting about how many homes they owned on various exotic islands. Even though this company was a much smaller company than Toyota, these board members acted like royalty.

In order to be successful, organizations must be a team of engaged and effective employees who enjoy their jobs and are committed to providing input to continually improve systems, procedures, and operations. Only then will customers fall in love with the organization long term.

One important difference identified in the Employee Induction Motor is that in the new global economy it has become very important for organizations to account for and balance the interaction of both employees and systems with customers. Today businesses need to marry systems and employees to continually improve interaction with customers. Input from every employee is needed if an organization is going to surpass the new global competition. There is little room for error today – both good and bad news travels very fast. Integrating very powerful and rapidly changing information systems into an organization is extremely complicated, and it is critical to get it right to be successful in today's world.

Not long ago, the only way to communicate with customer or anyone outside of the organization was by landline phone, in person, or by letter. Today we have an astounding number of choices including cell phones, smart phones, e-mail, voice mail, text messages, web pages, and business-to-business computer networking. The two-way arrow under "Systems" in the Employee Induction Motor diagram below has only existed strongly for the last few decades. How well organizations merge customer interaction with systems and employees is the key to success in today's world. Organizations also need to ensure they do not allow new systems to destroy traditional customer contact represented by the two-way arrow under "Employees" on the left side of the Employee Induction Motor.

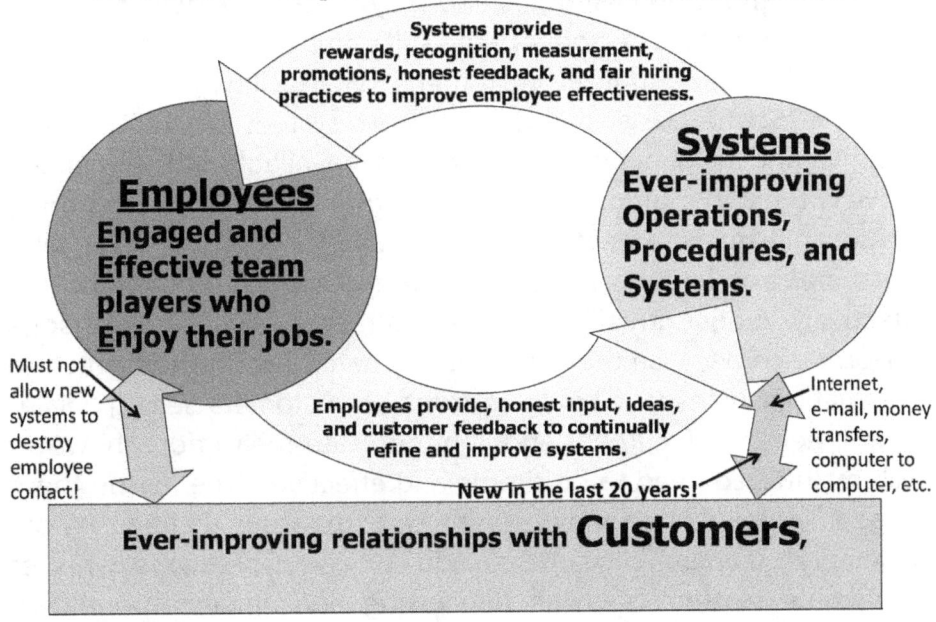

Companies today seem to struggle to merge all these tremendous improvements in computer technology and information management in an effort to create and maintain ecstatic customers. This is such a complex task that it takes input and cooperation from everyone in the organization to stay ahead of the new global competition. Today more than ever it takes a true team effort and one leader barking orders cannot be successful long-term.

I think everyone has witnessed companies making serious errors as the information age has progressed. In many organizations it is almost impossible to actually speak with or communicate directly with an employee. Everything is voice prompts, voice mails, or email. One of the reasons the chemical distribution company I worked for decided to centralize its customer service personnel was the belief that it was too costly to maintain seventy different computer systems in seventy locations. In my opinion management guessed wrong. With the advent of the internet there is less of a need to centralize employees. Their new system to centralize customer service negatively impacted customers and may have even increased costs because some office personnel were still required at field locations to interact with the centralized customer service facility.

In 1985, the paper-based call-report system we utilized was effective, and the paper records were readily available and permanent. I have witnessed multiple organizations that implemented customer relationship management (CRM) programs for their traveling sales personnel, and in almost every case, the systems did not work very effectively. Frequently these systems detracted from a sales person's performance because they were sitting behind computers entering information instead of being in front of customers selling. Sales people need to document and communicate their efforts however systems utilized need to be simple and effective. One reason these types of systems frequently turn into albatrosses is that as they are developed, leadership wants to add a million bells and whistles to provide features such as forecasting and linking information about prospective customers with existing accounts, actual orders, and revenue. Systems can became so cumbersome they drag organizations down instead of providing any real benefit.

I have witnessed many organizations that have implemented voice mail, automated phone menus, and web-based systems in an attempt to decrease the number of customer service personnel and supposedly save money. Customers of these companies are frequently so frustrated that they instead call their sales representatives to get anything done. The sales representatives are now on their smart phones most of the day handling customer service activities instead of calling on new potential customers.

Effective companies like Southwest Airlines somehow manage to quickly answer the phone when customers call to order tickets while also offering one of the best services available to make reservation online. Compare that to calling a company, going through umpteen prompts by touching one button after another, and hearing the recorded message "Your call is very important to us. However all of our customer service agents are busy assisting other customers. Your call will be answered in approximately twenty minutes." Southwest has somehow utilized enough input from employees to build systems that allow excellent service through the traditional and new arrows in the Employee Induction Motor. I have no doubt Southwest also uses these systems to seamlessly interact with vendors, regulators, and the community as we will discuss in the next chapter.

Southwest Airline's recent change in their boarding policy is a good example of being evolutionary instead of revolutionary. As a business traveler, I liked Southwest's prices and dependability, but I did not like having to arrive at the airport early to obtain a plastic boarding card to avoid being assigned a middle seat. Instead of scrapping their open seating policy, Southwest eventually implemented a system that allows passengers to obtain a boarding pass on their website twenty-four hours before departure. While retaining the efficiency of open seating, Southwest is providing improved service to customers. I am sure that this change evolved from employee ideas that were based on close interaction with customers.

Our nationwide environmental business unit we created inside of the chemical distribution company was one of the first companies to provide our truck drivers with cell phones and portable fax machines. Our customer service personnel were in constant contact with the drivers and the fax machines allowed them to fax examples of correctly completed manifests and other documents to our drivers to ensure all paperwork was accurate. One bit of technology that we did not allow during normal business hours was the use of voice mail for incoming calls, as we felt it was critical for all customer calls to be answered personally during business hours.

This book is also an excellent example of how companies can seamlessly merge employees, systems, and new technology to provide outstanding products and services to customers. When I decided to write a book, I was not sure where to turn. I met a local publisher at a conference, and we began to proceed down the road of publishing this book. My contact showed me some of their work, and they definitely produced nice quality books. To receive a competitive price, the minimum print run for a paperback book was 1,500 copies. I asked how they would help market the book and was told that they would give me a packet of information with some pointers on how to get the book in bookstores and on Amazon.com. They told me that I would have to do most of the work myself. I am passionate about the message of this book and plan to push the concepts of this book until I lose my voice, but I was concerned about how well I could market the book on my own as well as how quickly I could sell the initial 1,500 copies. I did not want a stack of books sitting around getting musty while I tried to sell them. Also, I had spent many years overseeing marketing departments that produced tens of thousands of brochures and then had to throw thousands away when a change needed to be made. Consequently I have been a big fan of print on demand for many years.

I was exploring alternative publishing options when I left an e-mail message at the *CreateSpace* Web site, which is owned by Amazon.com. That was on a Sunday. On Monday, I received a call from Jenny of *CreateSpace*, and we spoke for forty-five minutes about all aspects of the editing and layout services offered. In addition to editing, layout, and publishing, *CreateSpace* also provided a one-hour consultation with a marketing expert who has personally published multiple successful business books. As soon as the book is published, it would be sold through Amazon. Most importantly, after the very reasonable initial investment, I could order books, 100 at a time, for roughly 50 percent of the per-book price it would have cost me to order 1,500 at a time though the local publisher. Jenny also told me that if I decided to modify less than 10 percent of the content, the price to update the book was relatively insignificant.

I felt bad about not doing business with the local publisher, but I couldn't ignore the fact that *CreateSpace* had merged new technology with employees and systems in a way that provided far superior products and services. *CreateSpace's* presence on the Internet allowed me to find it, but it was the direct personal contact and sincere interest in my project that helped complete the sale. The clincher for me is that *CreateSpace* offered the latest technology with on-demand printing, which ensures better pricing and zero waste. When I call or e-mail Jenny, I always receive an immediate response, and during our first conversation I learned that she was from Charleston, S.C. Fifteen years ago my wife and I were guests at a Charleston restaurant that had a five-course dinner and a singing chef and staff. Although we loved the evening, we could not remember the restaurant's name. I asked Jenny about it, and she knew exactly which restaurant I was talking about. She even sent me a link to the restaurant's Web site. That is the kind of personal service that creates loyal customers. I have since received the same kind of employee and system driven customer service from companies like Tire Rack, GoDaddy, Quickbooks Online, and Salesforce.com.

To excel, a great team of employees in a well-run organization needs to stay focused on maintaining and creating ecstatic customers who like - or even love - their organization better than the competition. This is how organizations continue to grow profitably. As I've mentioned, it takes a considerable amount of effort and input from all employees and customers. All employees need to continually ask for and listen to customer input, and systems can be put in place to encourage this exchange. Customer feedback e-mails and phone numbers can easily be created for employees and customers to utilize. Employees should be encouraged to report all customer feedback, both good and bad. Positive comments by customers need to be broadcast to employees, and employees who provide this input need to be recognized. These types of systems help build morale. In chapter 16 we will discuss an employee input/recognition system that can be easily created in any company.

It is also important to create a culture where negative customer feedback is addressed. One of the most difficult concepts for employees to grasp is that knowing about customer complaints is good! The only situation worse than an upset customer complaint is not knowing about the customer's complaint. The problem with complaints is that employees play the "blame" game or the "cover-my-butt" game. Even within well-run companies, it is difficult for employees to address customer complaints. When I was part of the Improvement, Communication and Recognition committee at Resin Recyclers, I recommended tracking and following up on customer complaints as well as analyzing lost accounts to determine why they were lost. The committee members just could not bring themselves to address either issue. At one point I asked about reviewing a large account that was lost because of a discrepancy over the type of waste received by Resin Recyclers. I brought up the past customer's name at a committee meeting, and it was as if I lobbed a hand grenade into the room. Senior managers were yelling that this customer screwed us, and refused to talk about that account any longer.

The reaction some employees have to honestly addressing serious customer complaints and problems makes me think of when I recently spoke with Len Harvey, the retired President of Borg-Warner Chemicals, where I worked during the summers while going to college. When I asked Mr. Harvey why he was so successful he simply explained that he did not want employees to be afraid to make a mistake. Making an honest mistake is generally okay; real problems are created when employees are afraid to own up to mistakes, cover up their mistakes, or do not forgive fellow employees when they make an honest mistake. When it comes to dealing with negative customer feedback, all employees need some pretty thick skin.

It is my understanding that many years ago Japanese car companies began tracking repairs under warranty to determine what was failing. The idea was to continually eliminate the problems at the top of the list. I remember when I received an American-made company car in the early 1980s it was routine to take it back to the dealer five to ten times for repairs before the 12,000-mile warranty expired. I am not sure if these companies were tracking warranty problems or not, however the quality of the cars was certainly not improving at the time.

When I present the Employee Induction Motor model, some leaders tell me that they see customers as being part of their organization. It has also become popular lately to "fire" customers who are not profitable. From my experience both of these ideas are off target.

First of all, regardless of what kind of contract or relationship an organization has with a customer, you are never married forever. The contract can be broken, and you can end up in a nasty divorce and not speak for a very long time. Customers are not part of your organization and can never be taken for granted. Your organization is only dating your customers and needs to treat them as though it's early in the courtship. In the same way you buy flowers or make a special dinner for your date, organizations need to always make their customers feel special.

The idea of firing a customer is equally ridiculous. When I was working for one environmental company, I called on a customer that had been "fired," but now the company wanted to resume doing business with them. The buyers I met with felt as if they had been fired, and I was sure it would be many years before we would do business with them again.

Remember, you are never married to your customer

- You must <u>treat customers like you are on a date</u> to keep them "in love" with your organization.

- Customers <u>will hate you</u> if they call and all they hear is:
  - Voice mail
  - "Push 1 for.., Push 2 for..."
  - "To expedite your order visit our web page..."

  Successful organizations <u>seamlessly merge employees, systems, and new technology</u>.

- If you have to "break up" with a customer, <u>agree to disagree as amicably as possible</u>. You might want to "date" them again.

There are times it makes sense to "agree to disagree." There is nothing wrong with your price being too high or being unable to offer a service to a customer. It never makes sense to do business with a customer if the arrangement is not beneficial to both parties. If an arrangement is not mutually advantageous, the goal is to break up with a customer as gently as possible. You never know when you will want to do business with them again. You also don't know if that person will transfer to a different organization and sour your relationship there as well.

After only a few months as a branch manager at the chemical distribution company, I realized that it would be impossible to make money if I said yes to every deal. Not every deal is a good deal, and I decided there is absolutely nothing wrong with saying no, it is simply a matter of being as diplomatic as possible.

It takes a tremendous amount of honesty within an organization for customers to fall in love with the organization. This takes a continued effort that must come from the top, since senior managers cannot be above taking responsibility for their actions. Leaders are human, too, and employees have no problem with an honest mistake. Employees can quickly become zombies working for leaders who refuse to admit and take responsibility for honest mistakes.

Chapter 8
Vendors, Regulators, and Outside Influences

Understanding how your organization interacts with vendors, regulators, the community, our planet's environment, and other outside influences is also extremely important to maintaining a well-run business. In 1985 when I worked with North American car companies, they treated vendors as if they were the enemy. They would go out for bid, and the lowest price was rewarded with the business regardless of what assets the vendor had dedicated to servicing their account. One time we delivered a truckload of a chlorinated solvent known to cause significant ground contamination if spilled. An employee at the car company instructed our driver to hook the hose up to a specific line that was clearly labeled for the product being delivered. Our driver did as told, and once he pumped the 4,000 gallons off the truck he began to smell the solvent. It turned out that the line had been disconnected about 300 feet away and the entire load had been pumped on the ground. The plant manager brought us into his office and demanded that we pay for the cleanup even though our driver was following their employee's instructions. Contrast that to the management philosophy of companies like Honda and Toyota, which work hand-in-hand with vendors to allow both parties to continue to become more efficient, and both parties take responsibility.

In the 1970s and the 1980s, most of the companies with which I worked also seemed to treat both regulators and the community as enemies. Organizations appeared as if they had the right to contaminate the environment if it was good for their business. Environmentalists were labeled as fanatical tree-huggers bent on ruining legitimate businesses. When we decided that the number one unwavering principle at our environmental business would be to do the right thing and abide by and work with the regulatory community, we set the stage to reap unimagined benefits. For example, this created tremendous positive energy with employees, customers, and the community. We really meant what we said, and we proved it with our actions.

Today I have witnessed hazardous waste incinerators that provide direct communication from the process control computers to the regulatory community, allowing regulators to monitor all aspects of the operation twenty-four hours a day. By building systems and philosophies that work hand-in-hand with regulatory agencies, the environment, and vendors, organizations can help themselves prosper dramatically and still keep everyone happy.

It remains very popular for industry representatives to push for deregulation, believing that almost all regulation inhibits the ability to be competitive. These people want to return to the good old days, when businesses could do whatever they wanted. Those times are long gone. In a global economy, regulations and guidelines by which all must abide will increase, and countries and organizations that recognize this and work within these new restrictions will prosper while those that continue to go against the grain will suffer.

This is not to say that businesses should roll over every time a new regulation is passed. Organizations and specific industries need to cooperate in order to ensure new regulations are realistic and will benefit everyone over time - not just themselves in the short-term. Today it should be about efficient and effective regulations that encourage sustainable business. Eliminate outdated regulations and create new regulations that encourages a strong and successful

globally competitive economy and country. zDoing the right thing is always the correct direction to take, even if it hurts temporarily. Trying to change regulations so that your industry or organization can still sell buggy whips has always been a recipe for disaster, yet it continues because of the desire for short-term gain. In time, this kind of thinking can destroy an organization or severely damage an entire industry.

For a great example of lack of regulation gone wrong, you need only look at the period between 1998 and 2008. In the late 1990s, a new financial instrument called a credit default swap was created for financial institutions to use as assets. As I understand it, this instrument is equivalent to insuring your neighbor's house. If the house burns down, you benefit. It is completely unregulated, and an unknown but potentially large portion of these credit default swaps are considered toxic assets and have little actual value. In the late 1990s, there were approximately $1 trillion dollars tied up in credit default swaps. Congress discussed regulating credit default swaps in 1999, but as deregulation became more popular, the idea disappeared. So by late 2008, credit default swaps in the United States had reached the $40 trillion mark (Snyder, 2008). Forty trillion dollars is roughly equivalent to the total market capitalization of every publicly traded company in the entire world as of September 2008. It is hard to believe that the Security and Exchange Commission, or even someone in the financial institutions, did not call attention to this and try to bring the situation under control. These toxic assets contributed to the collapse of our financial system in a heavily deregulated environment, and it will now take decades to straighten out.

Credit Default Swaps (CDS's) demonstrate the need for responsible regulations

- CDS's are <u>completely unregulated financial assets of questionable value</u> created in the late 1990's by financial institutions (toxic assets).

- 1998 to 2008 CDS's for U.S. financial institutions ballooned <u>from ***one trillion to forty trillion*** ($40,000,000,000,000.00) creating a long-term financial mess.</u>

- ***U.S. CDS's equal the total market capitalization of all the publically traded companies in the world*** as of September 2008.

Another example of companies who may have hurt themselves by fighting against regulations is North American auto manufacturer's battle against new mileage standards. For a long time, American car companies fought against increased mileage standards, but now they face bankruptcy. Car companies may have been able to avoid this situation had they been required to meet new and fair mileage standards that increased over time allowing them to produce cars with higher gas mileage that could be sold worldwide. In addition, a decrease in the dependence on foreign oil may have helped minimize the financial problems faced by our country in 2008 by reducing the additional burden created by sky-rocketing oil prices. In terms of complete deregulation, the old adage "be careful what you wish for" definitely applies. Having free rein to do it your way sounds great, but doing the right thing will always benefit your organization more in the long term.

Chapter 9
Four Unwavering Principles All Employees Know

Our environmental business unit was able to excel because of four fundamentals understood by all employees in the organization. When I took over the business, the number one goal of my management team was to improve compliance and ensure we did everything right. Our second fundamental was based on employees. Our small management team had a gut feeling that we could not make our customers ecstatic without having a team of motivated and empowered employees who truly enjoyed their jobs. Once we had a team of motivated employees doing the right thing we added our third fundamental - to make the customers ecstatic. Because we were a for-profit company, the final fundamental was to carefully manage our expenses and ensure that we are profitable in the long term. Only a year or so after these fundamentals were implemented, the environmental industry fell into a very severe recession, but these fundamentals allowed our environmental unit to flourish.

    We started every meeting with a brief review of these fundamentals. If you asked any employee, "What are the four objectives we are trying to accomplish?" he or she would respond with our fundamentals. We felt these fundamentals and the entire Employee Induction Motor were a permanent model of how our organization would operate

Four unwavering principles (In this order)

- **Rock solid foundation to do the right thing**, especially in regards to health, safety, the community, regulatory compliance, accounting, and the environment.

- **Every employee enjoys their job** by being engaged and effective team players.

- **Very ecstatic customers** is everyone's goal.

- **Steady profitable growth** is our continual objective, and everyone needs to be fiscally responsible.

regardless of the latest mission statement. The entire concept of constantly using employee input to improve, add, and change products and services requires this model to be fairly stable while everything else continues to improve.

Most importantly, our management team was committed to walk the walk. Early in my career, someone said, "It is not what you say, it is what you see." Leaders can write any kind of mission statement or core fundamentals, but employees are only going to believe what they see. I have witnessed many leaders in my career and in the news who have lost sight of doing the right thing:
- Enron and others who cooked the books when they began to fail financially.
- Companies that postdated stock options to generate personal wealth.
- Leaders paying $1.2 million to redecorate their office as their company is failing.

Four Unwavering Principles All Employees Know

The worst example with which I am familiar stays with me to this day. Because of my success obtaining new accounts while in my first sales position, I was promoted to branch manager of a chemical distribution facility in a small Midwestern town at only twenty-five-years old. I accepted the job, sight unseen, and was shocked when I saw the location, especially since the outgoing branch manager had been promoted due to his financial success at the operation. This manager had only been there for a year and a half, and he told me that his goal was to generate as much profit as possible so he could get promoted to a larger branch. He accomplished his goal, but at a price.

The place was filthy because he fired the cleaning service to save money. One of our drivers came in while my predecessor and I were talking and asked how much extra to add to the tank truck of solvent he had just delivered to one of our largest customers. "Add 600 gallons. They will never know," the outgoing manager responded. My predecessor told me that he kept track of the customers that did not have gauges on their tanks or scales at their facility. If customers did not have any way of measuring the chemicals delivered, he added fictitious product to the bill. He had ripped our customer off for $1,200.00, and he was proud of it. He told me that he instructed employees to fill 55 gallon drums to 42 gallons. He gave me yet more advice: "If someone complains, just tell them that the drum scale was off." This was a small location, and he had doubled the operating profit to $200,000 per year. Half of the profit was due to quarterly inventory *write-ons*, which would be impossible for a properly-run operation. I now had a dilemma - do I keep operating unethically and illegally, or do I jeopardize my career by immediately reducing the profitability of my facility? I did not know who to ask for advice, so I turned to my father. He told me that the first company for whom he worked was so unethical that he felt miserable working there. Eventually he found Borg-Warner Chemical and decided to spend the rest of his career there because they always operated ethically. I decided to correct the short shipments.

It was not long before the profit performance for my facility began to decline. My regional manager, who was also new at his position, began asking a lot of questions about our performance. He looked at the numbers and asked me about the inventory gains. I did not want to accuse the former manager, but what was I to do? My new boss was also an honest man, and he was furious when he learned what had occurred before I took over the facility. My regional manager told me he would talk to his superiors about possibly reprimanding the former manager. I am not sure what happened however it seemed like the situation just kind of faded away.

Over time we built a strong team at this small chemical distribution facility, and we all enjoyed working together. Performance began to pick up in all areas - this time for real, and the results felt immensely fulfilling. It is always important to succeed, however it is far more important and satisfying to succeed without any asterisks, and without leaving dirty footprints in your wake. In the end, all anyone is really left with is his or her personal legacy and peace of mind. Succeeding by doing the right thing is what gives people real net worth.

After a few years I was promoted again to manage a much larger chemical distribution facility in western New York. Like all organizations, the chemical distribution company I worked for employed mostly honest and hardworking people, and fortunately a relatively few acted dishonestly like the very deceptive previous manager. In contrast, my predecessor at the new location was one of the hardest working, most respected and honest people I have known, and we are still friends today.

Even though I am sure it was not intentional, after my transfer to a new location it still felt as if there was somewhat of a companywide culture to quietly cut corners in field operations, while spending massive amounts of money to maintain headquarters that resembled the Taj Mahal. When I arrived at my new facility in western New York the chemical storage tanks were poorly assembled and in desperate need of repair. Corporate management had not provided the previous manager with the funds to repaint the tanks, causing them to rust to the point of leaking. To save money the tanks were installed fifteen years earlier on top of four inches of non-reinforced concrete, which is the standard for a pedestrian sidewalk, not a tank that weighs 200,000 pounds when full of chemicals. When I arrived, the entire tank farm needed to be replaced. The tanks containing highly flammable and toxic chemicals were resting on the crumbling concrete like various versions of the Leaning Tower of Pisa, and many were unusable due to leaks.

Even when the tanks were replaced they continued to cut corners wherever possible. Instead of buying new tanks they patched the old tanks before placing them on the required 12 inches of reinforced concrete. To save more money corporate engineers buried the pipelines from the tanks to our drumming station instead of placing them in an accessible trench as I had requested. I did not want to be responsible for a facility with underground pipelines, and I was sure regulations would require them to be dug back up in the near future. Sure enough, within only a few years the company had to pay additional tens of thousands of dollars to dig up and replace the pipelines.

The issue of quietly cutting corners in field operations was finally brought to light when a million-gallon diesel fuel tank ruptured, sending 750,000 gallons of fuel into one of the nation's largest rivers. To save money, our parent company had cut up and moved the million-gallon storage tank from another location only to reassemble and patch it at the new location near the river. The tank had not been properly tested before it was filled with over five million pounds of diesel fuel. The tank ruptured like a giant water balloon, sending a huge oil slick down one of the nation's largest rivers, requiring many large cities to shut off the water supply to citizens. To save a few thousand dollars and not do the right thing, it ended up costing the company over $40 million and nearly bankrupted the entire organization.

Unfortunately, I have witnessed and read about too many organizations with leaders who have also turned our four unwavering principles upside down because of a short-term focus on making money quickly. The batting order for many organizations appears to be:

- Make **money** in the short term, even if it means making severe cuts that inhibit the ability to service customers.
- Take care of **customers** as best you can with what you have left.
- Put tremendous pressure on **employees** basically making their life miserable.
- **Do the right thing** only when it is convenient, and doesn't get in the way of profit.

We all work for money, but money alone is never going to make anyone happy. Contributing and enjoying our jobs feels a lot better than making a few more bucks for our company or ourselves by being unethical. The specific language of the four unwavering principles can be modified for an individual company.

Four Unwavering Principles

- **Rock solid foundation to do the right thing!**
  To provide the highest quality products and services, all employees must act with absolute integrity by always doing the right thing for our customers, community, and fellow employees. If we discover a mistake, honesty with our customers and fellow employees allows us to find solutions to ensure the same mistake does not reoccur. All activities must be in compliance with applicable regulations and always in a safe, clean, and responsible manner.

- **Engaged and effective employees enjoy their job**
  We can only perform at our best if we are hardworking, dedicated, empowered, and effective. We are part of a work

family that must recognize each other's accomplishments and support each other to execute goals as a unified team. We must not fear speaking our minds, and we must listen to others and not be offended by honest feedback. In this environment work is satisfying and fun.

- **Very ecstatic customers**
  We can only create ecstatic customers if we enjoy our jobs and strive for absolute integrity. Our goal is to be the very best in customer service and sales by exceeding our customer's expectations. We must listen and be empathetic with our customer's needs. It is our job to resolve the customer's problems or concerns while maintaining our own high quality and standards.

- **Steady profitable growth**
  By focusing on integrity, job satisfaction, creating long-term ecstatic customers, and operating efficiently, we can charge a fair price and provide a profitable return for our company. By having a healthy, vibrant, and growing company of employees that enjoy what they do for a living, the employees, customers, investors, and community mutually benefit long-term.

Chapter 10
You Can't Fake It!

After working with many companies, I really believe many leaders do not understand the importance of engaged and effective employees. Instead, they seem to feel they can make demands with little regard to what the employee's think.

Organizations can't fake it!

- As <u>humans</u> we are more perceptive than we realize.

- As <u>customers</u> we generally know if an organization is not an effective, engaged team that enjoys what they do for a living.

- As regulators, a member of the community, or other outside influences <u>we also know</u>.

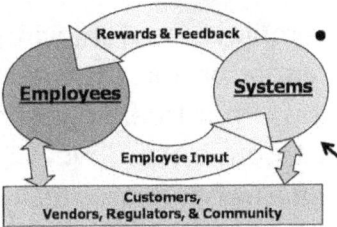

Customers gravitate to the most effective organizations!

I have read many studies on the importance of body language and voice inflection in making a sale and keeping the customer happy. Some studies have even stated that 50 percent of a successful sale can be attributed to body language and 30 percent to tone of voice, while other studies have suggested that as much 80 percent of successful phone transactions are due to the tone of voice (Sherwood, 1986). Now studies are even looking at the importance of digital body language or tone in e-mails and texts. I have heard it said many times that people should smile while they are talking on the phone because the person they are talking to senses that they are smiling.

The problem with simply telling someone to smile or improve their body language is that people are so perceptive that over time we can tell when a smile is fake, even over the phone. While understanding body language is important, it is very difficult for sales people to be effective without a high level of true confidence and belief in their organization. Just like a date that is not honest about themselves, organizations cannot fake it for long. Sales people need to also be part of the team and not blame everything on their team members. Sales people need to buy into their organization and find ways to believe in and help improve their support team.

By now, you know how impressed I am by Southwest Airlines. As I travel, I have asked many Southwest Airlines employees from all levels of the company what they think of their employer. Each time I've been told that Southwest is a great company for which to work! Considering that I must have spoken with thirty to forty employees, I am amazed that I did not run across at least a few disgruntled people, but this enthusiasm seems typical of Southwest Airlines personnel (Grubbs-West, 2005).

Once, a business leader told me that "If my employees are enjoying what they are doing for a living, then I am either paying them too much or they are screwing off." Obviously this is not true, however it does make the point that it is important to understand what it means for employees to enjoy what they do for a living. People really do want to be effective, and they want to be part of a positive work family. The idea of the Employee Induction Motor is to provide a one page visual model where this is a constant.

On the reverse end of the spectrum, a business can also sabotage its success by cultivating the wrong values. Buyers will quickly perceive underhanded tactics and values and decide to take their business elsewhere. When I began working as a consultant for a recreational vehicle (RV) dealership, the sales manager handed me a book that he said many car dealers believe is "the bible of car sales." It was a training book for car salespeople, and it literally made me sick to my stomach because it seemed to advocate being dishonest. The book instructed salespeople to sneer and talk about the bad condition of the client's current car when determining its worth. This book advised that training sessions never exceed thirty minutes because that was the limit of a car salesperson's attention span. I am certainly in favor of concise meetings and believe they should generally be no more than one to two hours long, but to assume that the people you have hired cannot sit still for more than thirty minutes does not send a very positive message to employees. According to this book, sincerity and doing the right thing seemed pretty far down on the list. It is no wonder people have become frustrated with traditional car salespeople. This is a far cry from the message companies like Southwest give to their employees. Fortunately the RV dealer did not abide by this manual and instead worked in the best interest of the customer.

Great organizations like Southwest Airline, Honda, and Toyota create a very positive culture. This type of culture keeps customers coming back and also allows employees to stay positive even during difficult times. I am sure everything has not always been a bed of roses for these organizations; however, their positive organizational culture has allowed them to continually provide superior service to customers and continued financial success regardless of any day-to-day issues they may be facing.

Chapter 11
The Complete Employee Induction Motor

Many companies offer one message for employees, another for regulators or the environment, another for vendors, and yet another for the community. The Employee Induction Motor is designed to provide a single message for everyone. There is no need to apologize for being a for-profit company, if you abide by the rules and take good care of your employees and customers.

What we found when utilizing the Employee Induction Motor was that performance improved in all areas, including long-term financial performance. Although placing doing the right thing, employees, and customers before making money may sound risky, the return will be more than worth your effort. Buyers will pay an average of a few percent more for better products or services, and volume growth of ten percent per year is very realistic for a company offering outstanding products and services from engaged and motivated employees. Likewise, a poorly run company full of zombies will generally need to charge a few percent less in order to sell their products and services and can often expect volumes to fall. I refer to this as the *ten and two rule* and the following hypothetical profit statement illustrates how a 2% change in price and a 10% change in volume can dramatically affect a company's financial performance.

The complete Employee Induction Motor

Systems provide rewards, recognition, measurement, promotions, honest feedback, and fair hiring practices to improve employee effectiveness.

Employees
Engaged and **E**ffective **team** players who **E**njoy their jobs.

Employee Induction Motor™

Systems
Ever-improving Operations, Procedures, and Systems.

Employees provide, honest input, ideas, and customer feedback to continually refine and improve systems.

Ever-improving relationships with Customers, Vendors, Regulators, Community, Investors, and Environment.

Rock solid foundation to do the right thing!
To provide the highest quality products and services, all employees must act with absolute integrity by always doing the right thing for our customers, community, and fellow employees. If we discover a mistake, honesty with our customers and fellow employees allows us to find solutions to ensure the same mistake does not reoccur. All activities must be in compliance with applicable regulations and always in a safe, clean, and responsible manner.

Engaged and effective employees enjoy their job
We can only perform at our best if we are hardworking, dedicated, empowered, and effective. We are part of a work family must recognize each other's accomplishments and support each other, to execute as a unified team. We must not fear speaking our minds, and we must listen to others and not be offended by honest feedback. In this environment work is satisfying and fun.

Very ecstatic customers
We can only create ecstatic customers if we enjoy our jobs and strive for absolute integrity. Our goal is to be the very best in customer service and sales by exceeding our customer's expectations. We must listen and be empathetic with our customer's needs. It is our job to resolve the customer's problems or concerns while maintaining our own high quality and standards.

Steady profitable growth
By focusing on integrity, job satisfaction, creating long-term ecstatic customers, and operating efficiently we can charge a fair price and provide a profitable return for our company. By having a healthy, vibrant, and growing company of employees that enjoy what they do for a living, the employees, customers, investors, and community mutually benefit long-term.

What is 2% in price and 10% in volume worth?

Impact on a hypothetical profit statement (1,000's)

	Original Profit and Loss Statement	2% Lower Average Prices	2% Higher Average Prices	2% Lower Average Prices and a 10% Decrease in Volume	2% Higher Average Prices and a 10% Increase in Volume
Gross Sales	15,000	14,700	15,300	13,230	16,830
Cost of Goods	11,250	11,250	11,250	10,125	12,375
Gross Profit	3,750	3,450	4,050	3,105	4,455
Fixed Cost	-2,250	-2,250	-2,250	-2,250	-2,250
Vaiarble Cost	-1,050	-1,050	-1,050	-945	-1,155
Net Profit	450	150	750	-90	1,050

500% more net profit → Strong profit as opposed to failure

In this example, a 2% change in average price up or down equals a 500% difference in operating income. When a 10% change in volume is also added, the difference is strong financial performance versus financial failure. It has been my experience that this is the actual environment that most businesses operate within, and the only way to succeed long-term is with an organization of engaged and effective employees who enjoy their work. When I was managing industrial chemical distribution facilities I quickly realized that a slight change in our gross margin and our expenses was the difference between successful and poor financial performance, and we needed to act as one team to ensure success.

Employee Effectiveness Systems

Chapter 12
Employee Induction Motor Training and Systems

In order for the Employee Induction Motor to be successful it takes a commitment from all leaders within an organization. A single leader who acts as if "it is my way or the highway" can ruin an employee-oriented atmosphere and negatively impact overall employee and organizational effectiveness. In addition to the commitment from leaders, the concepts of the Employee Induction Motor also need to be built into the systems of an organization. This final section discusses systems I have witnessed to be effective in promoting the concepts of the Employee Induction Motor. Obviously these systems can be modified and improved upon to work within your organization, and

I have included these examples to provoke thought about how they can be utilized to reinforce an employee-oriented culture.

One of the key aspects of the Employee Induction Motor is to point out that the human resources within a company determine how employees are hired, integrated, rewarded, recognized, measured, and evaluated. All managers must realize that perhaps the most important systems are those designed to determine hiring procedures, job titles, job descriptions, pay levels, bonus structures, recognition programs, measurement tools, performance appraisals, and discipline procedures for employees.

From my experience, companies of all sizes seem to view human resources as a necessary evil. Managers only bring in human resources personnel when they need "police" action to deal with an employee problem or to fire someone. Training programs for employees are reduced to the absolute basics. In my twenty years in management, I am sure I received less than one week combined of any real HR training. I can recall one day of candidate interview training, one day of reward/discipline training, and a few days of training regarding how to avoid different harassment situations. Many organizations state that employees are their most important assets, but focus few resources and little effort on providing systems to support employees. To compound matters, human resources departments are often understaffed and isolated from day-to-day company management.

When I first became a manager I spent less than a week shadowing the previous supervisor. That was my only introduction to management before taking on full responsibilities. In hindsight, I would have been an infinitely better manager had I even been provided with a week of Employee and Leadership training covered in the content in the following chapters.

If an organization chooses to adopt the Employee Induction Motor all managers need to attend leadership training specific to the objectives of the Employee Induction Motor. Managers need to understand the leadership paradox: if they feel they are a perfect manager, they most likely are not. New managers need to understand it is more about their employees than themselves, and instead of immediately demanding many changes, new managers need to ask a lot of questions of their new subordinates including:

- Tell me about your work experiences and background?
- Tell me about your current position?
- What can be done to help you do your job better? How can I help?
- If this was your company, what would you do to make us better?
- What are your career aspirations? How do you plan to achieve them? What can I do to help?

I would highly recommend that leaders within any organization utilize an interview process similar to the team interview process identified in the next chapter. Most of the organizations I have worked with do a poor job of interviewing and integrating new employees into the company. A structured team interview process helps improve the odds of choosing an employee who will be a good fit for the organization, and the process also helps recognize members who have been selected to be on the team. In addition to the reward of being asked to help select new employees, members of the interview team are now also committed to the success of the new individual they helped select. It is also very important that all new employees receive initiation training after joining the organization in order for everyone to understand the basics of Employee Induction Motor as well as the company's unique philosophies and culture.

Chapter 13
Hiring and Integrating New Employees

There are few responsibilities more important to an organization than hiring and integrating the right personnel, but many organizations use a slap-dash approach to these functions. Often when I have been interviewed for a job, the interviewer seemed to just wing it. He would ask a few questions about my college experience and then the interview would devolve into a discussion of sports or television. One of my sons recently interviewed for a job at one of the nation's largest soda manufacturers. The interviewer asked him to name his favorite movie and the last book he had read. He got the job, but, based on the interview, he is still not sure why.

Hiring is an area where a good system can greatly improve the quality of personnel brought into an organization. From my experience, I believe a structured team interview approach yields the most successful outcome. It allows the review of three or four candidates by the same group of employees in a one or two day. A sophisticated hiring system can even help attract better employees. I have had many very successful employees who went through a team interview tell me that they accepted the position because they were so impressed by the hiring process.

Do not just "wing it" when interviewing

Unfortunately, people are complex and no process is perfect. Even with a thorough interview process, it is possible to hire an employee who does not work out, however combining a structured interview process with the Employee Induction Motor leadership model will greatly improve the odds of hiring people who will be successful, engaged, and effective employees.

Structured Team Interview Process:
- The hiring manager should do the initial interviews and winnow candidates to three if possible. The hiring manager should then set up a team to interview all the candidates on a scheduled day or two. In general the hiring manager should not sit in on the panel and should instead allow the panel to be a separate evaluation of the candidates. It is not absolutely necessary that you use the same team for all candidates. Over time different teams will come up with similar results as everyone gets more used to the system.

Hiring

- Hiring manager interviews candidates and develops a list of at least three.

- A team of at least three additional employees interviews candidates separately on the same day if possible.

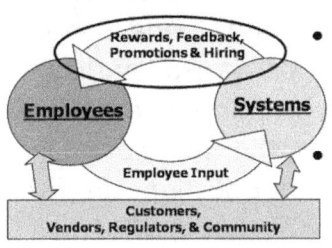

- A standardized format and scoring is utilized.

- Strong candidates are impressed by a strong interview process.

- The hiring manager should then select three or four key employees to be part of the team interview process. Assign one of them to be the team leader. It is best if several of the employees on the team are people who will work with the prospective candidate. An example of the three people chosen for a team interview committee to hire a new sales person might include:
    - A sales manager who is a peer of the hiring manager.
    - A salesperson who will be a peer of the prospective candidate.
    - A customer service person who will be working with the prospective candidate, even if he is a subordinate of the person being hired.
- The team leader should let the candidate know that the intention is not for the team interview to be high pressure,

and that there are no wrong answers, per-se. The questions are designed to allow the team to get to know the candidate and for the candidate to get to know the company. Let them know some team members may take notes only to make sure they remember the key points, and that the goal is simply to determine how well they fit together. Also, although this may sound insignificant, make sure the candidate has something to drink; he will be talking a lot and will obviously be a bit nervous.

- The team leader will assign different sections to each team member. Team members will ask the series of questions from their section and always start with the first general open-ended question in each section. Be alert for a candidate's response that may answer questions you planned to ask later. There is no need to re-ask a question the interviewee has already answered. Also remember these questions are used as a guideline and should not be asked verbatim. The idea is to ensure your questions cover all of the areas in each section. There are several benefits to each person asking standardized questions:

    ○ All candidates are asked similar questions.
    ○ Everyone on the team hears the same answer. Frequently people asking the questions are so intent on posing questions that they do not fully listen to the answers.

- After all of the questions have been asked, ask the candidate if he has any questions for the team or if there is anything else he would like to say about himself.

- When the interview is concluded, the team leader should escort the candidate out and then return to rate the candidate.

- Everyone should rate the candidate individually without any discussion immediately after the introduction. The team leader will then record all scores on one sheet. Each rating area should be discussed with the objective of agreeing on a score for each area such as communication etc. Most of the discussions should be on the areas where there are large discrepancies on the scoring. Finally an average score for the interviewee should be agreed upon and entered in the box at the bottom on the far right. This process is not a mathematical average but an agreement by the group after everyone has discussed their ideas.

- After the team leader records a final score one final rating sheet is returned to the hiring manager. Make sure all of the other sheets are destroyed.

- The hiring manager should use the final rating sheet, coupled with what is known about the candidate, to make the hiring decision. If you know the candidate has a ten-year history of exceptional performance, then that would generally take precedence over the team's recommendation. In general the hiring manager should keep the final scoring sheet.

A structured interview process similar to this provides many benefits:

- At least three existing employees will be committed to the new hire's success because they helped decide if that person should be hired.

- One of the key areas employees cite as a reason to be satisfied about a job is when their input counts. This is what the lower arrow on the Employee Induction Motor is all about. What better input could an employee provide then helping to decide who is hired?

- Employees allowed to sit on the team feel recognized because they were chosen for an important task. This is what the top arrow on the Employee Induction Motor is all about.

- The new candidates are hired based on their ability to fit in and be productive, instead of just who they know and the raw skills they can bring to the table.

For your benefit, I have included an example of an actual team interview process. Each person on a team interview committee should be provided with a copy of the entire team interview process listed in the next few pages as a guide to use and a place to take notes during the process. This can be modified to fit your organization.

<u>TEAM INTERVIEW PROCESS - GENERAL</u>

Instructions to Individuals conducting the interview
    The team interview process is designed to be conducted by three to four employees in a group setting. It is important to encourage the candidate to relax as much as possible. The objective is to determine if the candidate is a good match for the position and if the company is a good match for the candidate. Before you begin, choose a leader for the interview process. There are five sections to the interview process (education, work experience, interpersonal skills, goal orientation and job knowledge) and the team leader needs to decide who will handle each section. Persons responsible for handling each section should informally ask enough of the questions listed in each section to obtain answers to the questions in the section. **It is very important to start with the first open-ended question in each section.** Candidates may answer many of the following questions by answering this first

open-ended question. Feel free to take notes during the interview process.

The interview should take an hour or so. Once the interview is complete, someone should escort the candidate out of the conference room. Each interviewer should complete their initial assessment independently immediately after the interview. Once complete, the leader should fill in the ratings each interviewer gave the candidate and then review each section in the ratings to gain consensus. Once this is complete, the team needs to make a recommendation on whether or not to hire the individual.

Our goal is to staff our organization with the highest quality individuals we can hire, who meet the expectations of each specific position and the expectations of our company. We are looking for candidates that will be valued team members who will not allow their personal ego to get in the way of the team's success.

Note to individuals conducting the interview: Please do not ask about religion, age, marriage, children (including whether the candidate is planning a family), or personal information including height and weight, credit references, arrest records, or membership in clubs (unless professionally related).

Introduction to the Candidate

You should use something similar to the following introduction:

Thank you for participating in our team interview process. Please relax. Our objective is to ensure that you are a good match for our organization and that our organization is a good match for you. There are no patently wrong answers; we are simply attempting to give you every opportunity to help us assess how your talents and skills fit the available opening.

Some of us may take notes during the process. Please do not be concerned, this is to make sure we remember information in order to make a fair assessment.

To allow you to know whom you are talking with we would like to introduce ourselves to you. Our positions with the company are _____.

May I get you a soda or glass of water before we begin?"

1. Education (Note to hiring manager: You are required to contact universities or obtain a transcript to confirm degrees. Also, this section is much more important for more recent graduates.)

We know you attended_____, however, could you please give us an overview of your education?

How did you choose your major and minor?

What was your greatest accomplishment during your education?

What was your greatest disappointment during your education?

Tell us from start to finish about a major project with which you were involved during college. How did you decide on that project? How many people were involved? What did you learn?

What courses did you enjoy the most?

What courses did you enjoy the least?

How did your education experience prepare you for the _____ position for which you are applying?

2. Work experience

Could you give us an overview of your experience in your most recent position at _____, and could you give us an overview of the various positions you have held since you have been in the job market?

Could you tell us specifically what you did when you worked for_____?

What job did you enjoy the most? Why?

What job did you enjoy the least? Why?

Tell us from start to finish about a major project with which you were involved during your work career? How were you assigned that project? How many people were involved? What did you learn? What would you do differently?

Have you had any leadership roles? Could you tell us about those? What strategies did you find worked best?

What has been your greatest career accomplishment to date?

What has been your greatest disappointment?

Why did you decide to work for_____?

Why are you considering employment elsewhere?

If we asked your supervisor what kind of an employee you are, what would he say?

3. Interpersonal skills/do the right thing

How would you describe the way you interact with people with whom you work?

Give us an example of a conflict you had with a coworker. How did you handle it?

Give us an example of an honest mistake you made and explain how you handled it.

Without providing the person's name, give us an example of an incident when a coworker made an honest mistake that affected you and explain how you handled that situation.

What makes you angry? What do you do when you become angry?

With what type of person do you like to work?

With what kind of person do you least like to work?

How do you feel about compliance to regulations when it comes to satisfying a customer?

How do you feel about protecting the environment when running a business?

Tell us how you feel about your own ego. What makes you feel good about yourself?

Tell us about your hobbies and interests outside of work (please do not discuss activities involving a religious organization)?

4. Goal Orientation

Where do you see yourself in two years? In five years?

Do you set goals for yourself? What kind of goals do you set?

What do you think you need to do to achieve these goals?

What strategies do you use when you do not achieve your goals? What do you find works best?

Give us an example of a time when you set a specific goal for yourself that you did not achieve and the strategies you utilized when you realized you would not achieve this goal.

5. Job Knowledge

Tell us specifically about any previous experience you have had in _____ positions similar to the position for which you are applying.

Why do you think you will be an exceptional employee within our organization in the position for which you are applying?

What strategies would you utilize or think you will utilize to be successful in the position for which you are applying?

If you have held a _____ position, what has been your greatest achievement in that position?

If you have held a _____ position, what was your biggest disappointment in that position?

What do you think you will like best about a career in _____ at our organization?

What do you think you will most dislike about a career in _____ at our organization?

How would you organize yourself to be most effective in a _____ position at our company?

How many hours a week do you expect to work?

How well do you understand the basic knowledge of the _____ position for which you are applying? Could you give us some examples?

Are you willing to move to new areas of the United States to take on new assignments? (This is not necessarily a requirement of this new position; this is simply information that may serve us in considering future positions for you.)

Interview Conclusion

We have asked a lot of questions of you, is there anything else you would like to tell us?

Do you have any questions you would like to ask us?

Thank you for your time. We will need a few minutes to wrap up. We will get back to you by _____ date.

After the Candidate is Escorted out of the Room

Once the interview is concluded, escort the candidate out of the room and then regroup to rate the candidate immediately after the interview. Each person should have a form similar to the one below. Team members should individually rate the candidate for each area without discussion. The leader should then record the scores from each team member onto one sheet. Each area should then be discussed by the group and an agreed upon score should be recorded on the right side of the form for each area. These are not mathematical averages but rather an agreement by the team. Time should be spent on areas where there is a significant difference in ratings of more than a few points. After each area has been discussed a final score will be agreed upon at the bottom right of the form and a hire, no-hire decision should be checked. The leader should return one completed form to the hiring manager. All other forms should be destroyed.

Repowering American Industry!

Ratings

Candidate's Name_____   Date_____

Make sure the candidate is escorted out of the room before you begin the rating process.

Each interviewer should complete the following assessment **independently** on their scoring sheet utilizing a 1-10 scoring system (10 is a definite hire and 1 indicates a very poor match for the position). Once complete, the leader should place interviewer's names at the top of each column and fill in the ratings each interviewer gave the candidate. The leader should review each section of the ratings to gain team consensus for that section. Once this is complete the team needs to make a recommendation on whether or not to hire the individual. The team leader should return his completed score sheet to the hiring manager and make sure all of the rest of the forms are destroyed.

Interviewer's Names					Consensus Score
Education-Does this candidate have the proper educational or equivalent experience to be successful?					
Work experience-Does this candidate have the proper work experience to be successful? Did they provide good reasons for job changes?					
Communication-Did this candidate clearly communicate his ideas? Did he follow through and finish his thoughts? Is this candidate a good listener?					
Goal Orientation-Does this candidate set goals and work to achieve them? How well does he adjust when goals are not met?					
Interpersonal Skills-Does this candidate deal well with fellow workers? With customers? Will this candidate share his					
Job Knowledge-Does this candidate understand the basic knowledge necessary to be successful in this position? If not, does he have the ability to acquire it quickly?					
Position Aptitude-Has this candidate been successful at a similar position? Does he have the aptitude to be successful?					
Work Ethic-How hard will this candidate work? Do past achievements indicate hard work?					
Sense of urgency-Did the examples the candidate gave indicate he works with a sense of urgency?					
Proficiency for position-sales, customer service, engineer, etc.					
Desire to be successful-Does this candidate need to be successful as a person?					
Overall rating-How do you think the candidate will perform overall?					
Team recommendation: ____We **should** hire this individual for a position at our company. ____We **should not** hire this person for a position at our company.					

Chapter 14
Improvement, Communication, and Recognition Committees

One of the problems I have witnessed within most organizations is that meetings are frequently not very effective. There are either very few meetings or too many drawn out meetings with very little accomplished. The end result is minimal actual progress, poor communications, and little recognition for employees who contribute. One of my biggest frustrations when I worked at the chemical distribution company is that I would sit in day-long meetings as part of the senior management team when perhaps five minutes of the entire day would actually have anything to do with my environmental business.

One of the most effective systems I am aware of utilizes a hierarchy of Improvement, Communication, and Recognition (ICR) committee meetings. The name conveys the three things that need to occur based on any meeting. The only reason to have a meeting is to improve something, there needs to be communication about the improvement, and the people who are responsible for the improvement need to be recognized. Although this may sound like a lot of time spent in meetings, if managed correctly the actual time commitment is minimal and the results are tremendous. At the top of the committee hierarchy is a companywide improvement, communication, and recognition committee. This committee will

Improvement, Communication, and Recognition (ICR) Committees

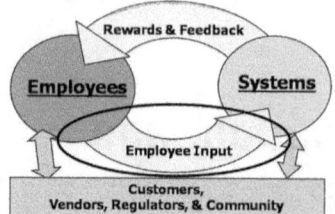 

- A corporate team is made up of 6-10 members from each different department or discipline (Operations, Sales, Accounting, HR, etc.)
- The team meet for an hour or so every other week with a crisp agenda.
- Issues that cannot be resolved are given to a subcommittee to work on and bring back to the ICR committee.
- Each department or location can also establish ICR teams that are represented by an individual on the corporate team.
- Well run ICR teams can improve almost any situation generally utilizing existing employees and available assets.

report to the president or organization leader; however the committee may or may not include this individual. This committee needs to abide by the same guidelines for all ICR sub-committees:

- A leader will be designated for each ICR committee who will be responsible for sending an agenda out to all members prior to meeting and sticking to the agenda during the meeting.
- The ICR committee leader will be responsible for ensuring meetings move at a rapid pace and are not dragged down by endless discussion with no progress. If a topic needs further discussion it will be assigned to a subcommittee who will report back at the next meeting.
- All members of ICR committees need to understand that they need to be concise in their communications and that they need to listen to the opinions of everyone. If a committee member

Improvement, Communication, and Recognition Committees

is constantly dominating the conversation and slowing down progress out of stubbornness, then they will be replaced.
- Someone will be assigned to take and distribute notes for every ICR committee.
- ICR committees have a tremendous amount of responsibility and need to delegate to subcommittees and members to ensure everything is accomplished. Among other assignments that will arise, the committee needs to review and address the following:
  - Approve the topics for a monthly newsletter for employees that communicates ICR improvement activities and recognition for employees who have contributed. Each department is also responsible for an article on employees in their department on a rotating basis (If there are twelve departments in the companywide committee, then each department is responsible for an article once per year).
  - All nominations for awards and suggestions for improvement will be reviewed and all employees receiving awards will also be printed in the company newsletter. The top ICR committee should make recommends to the president or organization leader regarding monetary rewards for truly outstanding achievements. Many of the recognition and awards will come from employee submittals of the input/recognition email/forms discussed in chapter 23.
  - A system will be put in place to track customer complaints and service failures. All customer complaints and service failures will be reviewed in ICR committees and followed up on. The goal of ICR committees is to modify systems and procedures so service and product failures do not reoccur. Employees who identify customer complaints and assist in providing solutions will be recognized and rewarded.

- All lost customers will be reported and analyzed by ICR committees and systems will be improved to ensure future customers are not lost.
- Representatives from each department will report on progress in their key areas.
- The human resources ICR committee, which would be better described as the "employee effectiveness" committee, needs to ensure systems are in place to continually improve employee effectiveness.

The number of ICR committees depends on the number of different departments and entities within an organization, and the topics covered are up to the committees. This may sound like a lot to cram into an hour and a half every other week, however I have seen it accomplished effectively. They key is to ensure that the right people are on each ICR committee and that they understand the need to be good listeners and concise communicators.

Chapter 15
Input and Honest Discussion Improves Almost Every Issue

It may be sounding a little like my mantra, but employee input really is what inspires fantastic morale and innovation. Leaders need to maintain rapport with all employees and seek out the truth about what needs to be done to continue improving. Managers should submit the input they have gathered and the names of employees who need recognition on a monthly basis to ICR committees.

Employee input is very important for identifying what new systems will solve large issues and how to plan for new products, facilities, and other major changes. When it comes to implementing improvements to systems, one of the problems I have witnessed is the "perfect is the enemy of good" syndrome, which occurs when a problem arises and a solution is postponed until new equipment arrives or can be purchased. This is especially true when it comes to computer systems and programs.

While planning for better future systems, it is continuous refinement *using existing systems* that makes the biggest difference for businesses on a day-to-day basis.

Honest employee input and discussion can almost always make a problem situation better using existing assets!

- New information and other systems may take forever to implement if organizations wait for perfection.

- Perfection can not be the enemy of good (good is way better than nothing).

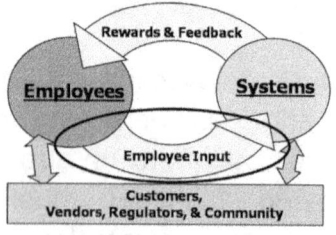

- Many problems can be resolved with excel, outlook, access, or even pen and paper until the perfect system arrives.

To give you an idea of what can be accomplished, I offer two examples I witnessed that were created from ICR committees where systems were dramatically improved utilizing existing assets:

Creating personnel training systems for a nationwide chemical waste collection organization operating out of eleven facilities.

As I discussed earlier, when we took over the small environmental business within a chemical distribution company, we were receiving fifty notices of serious violations per year. We made compliance our top priority and started every meeting with the idea of doing the right thing. Our compliance dramatically improved as we continued to refine how we ran the business. However, we continued to struggle with employee training.

Input and Honest Discussion Improves Almost Every Issue

Our organization had to comply with training requirements for eleven chemical waste storage permits, as well as a myriad of federal, local, and state regulations. That entailed more than forty different training courses that had to be conducted and documented annually for employees spread across the country. In our business, we were inspected frequently and without notice; if a complete list of training signed by all required employees could not be produced, inspectors would issue violations. In a busy, growing, and competitive business, even with minimal employee turnover, it was very difficult to keep up with 4,000 individual documented training courses per year (100 employees signing off on 100 training courses).

Our environmental business unit was supported by an environmental, health, and safety department that assisted the entire chemical distribution company. I asked the department head for help, and he told me that they were about to implement an amazing new computer system that would track training for all employees throughout the company. As the training violations mounted, I would contact that department only to be told the system would be installed in another about another six months. I soon realized this new system was always about six months away from being implemented.

My boss told me to fix the problem and suggested severely disciplining managers who did not document all training. Instead we formed a small team and brainstormed a solution to sort the training requirements into eleven stacks - each stack stood for one month. Training required by sales personnel who worked from home was set up every three months, when managers held their normal quarterly meetings. One of our assistants at corporate would send out a memo informing the manager which particular training requirements were due each month. (We already had all the training courses available on tape, and we had TVs and VCRs at all locations.) Each facility manager would have the employees sign local documentation that was kept locally with an additional copy sent back to corporate. If it was not received by the end of the month, I was advised, and I would tell them to complete the training regardless of how busy they were. This is why doing the right thing and employees come before customers, because if we were going to be able to serve customers in the future, the training requirements had to be met. This also really clarified our commitment to doing the right thing. If we had to hold customers off for a day to do the training in order to stay in compliance, that was preferable to bending the rules to take care of the customer in the short term.

This system utilized paper and about an hour of one person's time a month, and it rewarded us with perfect compliance. Even if training records were misplaced at the field office, we kept a duplicate copy at corporate that could be faxed to appease local inspectors. It was so successful that the entire chemical distribution company adopted it in place of the prophesied computer system that never materialized.

Developing an effective customer relationship management system using Microsoft Outlook

As I also discussed earlier, I have found that customer relationship management programs are a nightmare for many companies with traveling sales personnel. When I started in sales we were required to fill out a three-part call report form and send them to our managers for every significant call we made. While archaic by today's standards, it provided a record of what was happening with accounts. Amazingly, I have seen very few systems that have worked that well since the advent of computers, and I have even seen small and mid-sized companies simply go without any organized system. When I typed "failed customer relationship management programs" in Google, 569,000 results came up.

When I was consulting for one company, it was experiencing the same problem with its sixty-person sales and customer service team.

Several software programs had been purchased, tried, and then abandoned, and finally there was no system at all. While brainstorming with the head of their computer department, a few employees came up with a simple system that was implemented within a week. An e-mail address was created using Outlook called Sales Call Report. Because the entire sales force all had Blackberries, salespeople would simply send an e-mail to Sales Call Report and send a copy to their boss along with anyone else in the company who needed to take action as a result of the sales call. Because sales personnel generally sent an e-mail to someone in the company after each call, this system did not require any additional effort. The e-mail's subject line gave the company name, state, and city, and the e-mails were automatically distributed to folders sorted by sales manager. Soon the president, operations manager, and customer service manager were scanning these e-mails every day. I still think that, for a company of its size, this is an ideal system that cost nothing to implement and provided information in real time.

These are two small examples of how ICR committees using existing assets and systems. While solving day-today problems, these committees, and senior leadership, also need to think strategically about where investments in employees and systems need to be made to ensure long-term success. By improving issues using existing assets, while also strategically adding well thought out investments in systems and employees, organizations can continue to prosper long-term. The key is to continually gain as much employee input as possible.

Chapter 16
Employee Recognition Systems

A culture of recognition has to start at the top, and while many managers do not think about recognition in terms of systems, there are definitely systems that can be put into place to facilitate recognition, generally at a minimum cost. Some of the best forms of recognition I have experienced are a "good job certificate" signed by the president and article in the company newsletter. These are both easy systems to ensure recognition occurs on a regular, effective basis, but I have actually witnessed very few companies that have any formal systems in place to adequately recognize employees, or ask for employee input.

Recognition of fellow employees is a skill that is not reserved for managers. All personnel can positively contribute to an organization by recognizing coworkers for their contributions. In addition to being part of the Employee Induction Motor's Four Unwavering Principles, recognizing fellow employees can also be included in performance appraisals and the interview process.

I have found that one of the easiest ways to ensure employees provide input and receive recognition is to provide input/recognition forms and an e-mail address. The idea is that any employee who has an idea for improving something in the company simply fills out and submits the form or sends an e-mail. If the idea is printable it can be placed in the employee/customer newsletter. This way every person in the company has an opportunity to utilize this new idea. If substantial money is saved, leadership can reward the employee for the idea. Anyone who submits an idea will receive a coffee cup (or other items) and a thank you, or award certificate from the president or organization leader. All input and recognition recommendations go to the ICR committees who ensure that employees are properly recognized and rewarded. Every employee newsletter needs to include a copy of the form and the e-mail address to ensure input and recognition continues to be generated.

Create an email and form to allow employees to recognize others and to submit ideas for improvement

- Employees can provide an idea for improvement or recognize another employee for outstanding performance.

- Submittals are reviewed by the corporate ICR committee, and once approved the employees names, ideas, and reasons for being recognized are printed in the company newsletter.

- Employees receive a signed certificate from the president and additional compensation for exceptional ideas and achievements.

Companies can also use many other programs for recognition, such as the employee of the month program. The only caveat is that if leadership decides to implement any of these systems for recognition, they need to be fully implemented. If I had a dollar for every time

I walked into a customer's lobby only to see an employee of the month plaque that has not been updated for six months or more, I would have a tidy sum today. These actions send just one message to employees: "We started this program, but it is just not worth our effort to select an employee and buy a two dollar engraving plaque every month."

Chapter 17
Financial Rewards and Compensation

Another problem I have come across many times in my career is the assumption by management that compensation is unimportant since recognition is so important to employees. Even though employees do not work only for money, it is still the primary reason people seek and keep jobs. As a leader you should be perfectly aware that compensation is a critical part of ensuring employees enjoy what they do for a living. It is essential that compensation and bonus programs are fair and well considered. I have been amazed at how little thought is sometimes put into compensation and bonus programs even within very large companies.

Bonus and compensation programs must be designed to ensure all employees maintain the correct focus that will help achieve the company's ultimate goal. Often plans reward actions that are not in the company's best interest. For example, bonus programs often reward sales personnel for increased revenue, while bonus programs for operations and management personnel are based on profitability. Leaders complain that sales personnel sell at discounted prices, sell too many low-margin products or services, or sell to accounts with bad credit, but if you reward sales personnel only on revenue they will tend to sell any product to any account at any price, regardless of how little profitability is generated.

Because our environmental business unit was part a chemical distribution company, all sales reports included margin and revenue. Bonus programs for salespeople were based on increasing gross margin, while managers were rewarded on net margin because they had control of all expenses. Everyone was penalized for accounts that did not pay their bills. With this type of system, bonus programs were much more closely aligned with the goals of management. While we were extremely successful with this system in place twenty years ago, I have found that many of our competitors in the environmental industry still continue to reward sales personnel based solely on revenue, and still struggle with conflicting revenue versus profit goals between operations and sales.

I have consulted for some of these companies, and their leaders provide several reasons why they have not converted to a margin-based system. They say that sales personnel cannot be trusted with that information, and it is too difficult to calculate accurate costs to process waste materials. If employees are untrustworthy, than companies need to review their hiring process, and if costs are difficult to calculate, than managers cannot possibly be effectively running their businesses.

An ill-conceived bonus plan can completely demoralize a company, and yet I have seen companies implement plans with very little thought. When leaders realized the plans were flawed - usually when it was time to pay up - the solution was often not to pay the bonuses originally promised.

One of the companies I worked with seemed to have a habit of not paying bonuses as promised. Soon after I began working with them I was told about a sales representative that received only 30% of a huge bonus that was promised six years earlier. Apparently a senior manage sent a memo out saying that sales representatives would receive 1% of all large projects sold. Soon after the memo was distributed, the sales representative landed one of the largest projects in company history that generated $10 million of revenue and made a huge profit for the company. The sales representative fully expected $100,000 as promised, but the president decided the salesperson had not done enough work to earn the entire amount so the sales representative received only $35,000!

The betrayal was such a demoralizing event that employees are still talking about it fifteen years later and this cautionary tale is practically an initiation for all new employees. The assumption by many employees is that the company has shorted them on bonuses so often that all compensation programs should be viewed with extreme skepticism.

It's also important to recognize that if too much of an individual's compensation is derived from bonuses, some individuals' actions will be based on self-interest and they may be inclined to bend the rules to achieve adequate compensation. This is even true at the highest levels within an organization. A recent study by Moody's (Bertsch & Mann, 2005) found that "companies with the highest paid bosses, adjusted for things like company size and performance, were far more likely to default on debt or to suffer major cuts in bond ratings."

Up-to-date job descriptions (or some type of statements of responsibility) need to be in place for all employees and fair pay ranges have to be developed for these positions. A simple system to keep job descriptions up to date is to require employees to update their job description once a year when their performance review is due. Far too many small companies pay employees what they will accept instead of what they are worth based on their job description. I have witnessed companies that attract prospective employees by offering double the salary of current personnel in the same position. These types of pay inequities will only lead to poor morale and high turnover.

From my experience, larger companies often do not review job descriptions and payment structures frequently enough, with some jobs left unchanged for many years. I have worked with smaller companies where pay was completely unrelated to the job being performed and was instead tied to what the company felt was necessary to attract and retain each specific employee. When new employees were lured in with huge salaries leaders did not tell new employees that if their initial pay was too high they would probably never see a raise. This practice quickly demoralized employees causing them to either become zombies or leave.

Compensation needs to be fair

- Put the work up front into bonus and compensation plans so there are no disappointments later.

- Pay people what they are worth, make sure job descriptions are updated annually.

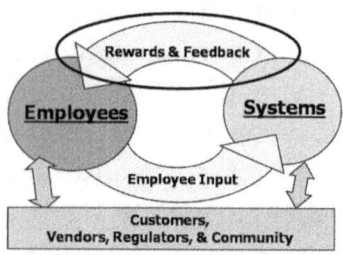

- Motivated, engaged, and effective employees are worth the money.

- If the company suffers everyone suffers to some degree.

All performance appraisals and job descriptions should also be reviewed by HR and perhaps an outside professional organization to ensure consistency in rating and pay structures. HR needs to have the resources and sophistication to evaluate pay based on the pay scales of other companies in the area and ensure that pay ranges are accurate based upon the work being performed.

Over time, large pay discrepancies cause companies to lose underpaid employees and keep overpaid employees who are not performing. This is a sure way to generate more zombies. Remember, the goal is for all employees to be engaged and effective because their input is being heard, they are being recognized, and they feel they are being paid fairly for their contributions.

Chapter 18
Employee Measurement Tools

Good measurement tools help separate *busy* work from *effective* work. As I mentioned in the previous chapter, all sales reports we utilized within our environmental business unit included gross margin by customer and product line (believe it or not, we had different product categories for various hazardous wastes we collected). While this is normal for businesses like retail and distribution, based on my experience it is rare for companies collecting and processing chemical waste. It allowed us to reward sales, customer service, and operations personnel on profit maintenance and improvement. It also allowed our entire organization to quickly understand the degree of profitability for each transaction.

Within our environmental business unit, we paired each customer service representative with one sales representative. Our idea was that a sales representative would be better able to bring in new accounts, while maintaining and expanding existing accounts because the customer service person would handle the day-to-day activities. Both were measured and rewarded based upon the increased overall margin for their territory.

Employee measurement tools

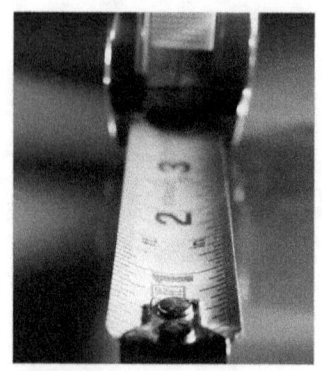

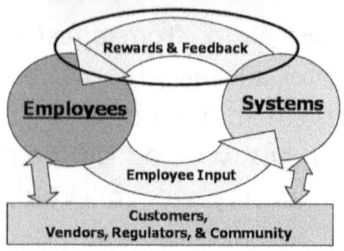

- Employees need to be measured on how effective they are, not how busy they are.

- Measurement tools need to ensure employees work towards the same goal – If sales is rewarded on revenue, and operations is rewarded on margin, there will be conflict.

Drivers were measured based on how many drums were collected per mile and per stop. From a corporate perspective, we quickly noticed that if our trucks became over 80 percent full, we started running out of room for growth. Because we were focused on customer service, our goal was to ensure that there was some extra room on the truck for customers that generated extra drums we did not expect. This satisfied the customers, and it also kept our costs in line because we did not need to send a second truck to pick up the unexpected drums. Our service was so strong compared to most of the competition that pricing became less important. Occasionally we would lose customers on price for one order only to later get them back permanently because our competitor could not match our service. I am aware of many competitors that were so preoccupied with keeping their trucks 100% full that their service suffered dramatically because they held off customers until their truck was full, or could not fit any extra unexpected drums on their truck.

Chapter 19
Promotions

Frequently, promotions within organizations suffer from the same "warm body" syndrome that can afflict the hiring process. This occurs when an opening arises and the first warm body that appears to have some approximation of the experience and qualifications needed is promoted into the position. Employees who felt they were qualified are left wondering why they were not even considered for the position. If the newly promoted manager is a poor leader, employees are also left to wonder why that specific person was selected.

Another issue is that some companies are constantly looking for a messiah from outside the company to come in and fix everything. In this scenario, leaders constantly look past all of the existing talent in the organization to find the "perfect" new manager or employee. Once again, this strategy will cause all employees to wonder why no one in-house was considered and why leadership picked this new individual.

For a period of time one of the companies I worked with subscribed to a cross-training program that sent managers from one business unit to a completely different business unit. Employees with specific knowledge did not understand why they were not considered for promotion especially when working for someone who did not have in depth knowledge in their department.

Promotions

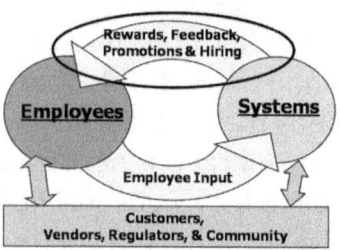

- Promoting qualified personnel is critical.

- To keep all employees motivated a fair system needs to be in place.

- All qualified internal candidates need to be considered and interviewed by an internal team, for all promotions.

    This company also decided that the planning and development department would be the grooming department for new senior-level executives. The company mostly overlooked the 100 or so field managers who consistently and successfully ran some of the most competitive businesses imaginable. Senior management decided they would send employees from planning and development away for a two-day testing program to determine if they would make strong executives. Those with high scores were put on a fast track for promotion regardless of their past experiences.

    Just before I left the company, I worked with a guy I will call Frank, who was in the planning and development department. Frank tested well at the two-day executive testing session, but I do not believe he had ever successfully managed anything in his career. Many managers, me included, were relatively unimpressed by his work while he was in the planning and development department. Frank lacked the experience and knowledge field managers gain through running ultra-competitive businesses for many years. Because Frank scored well on the two-day test, Frank was promoted to be the CEO's assistant. After serving as the CEO's assistant he was than given six-month stints in various managerial positions, and within a few years was promoted to president. It took years to measure a manager's effectiveness for the positions Frank was repeatedly assigned for only six months before being promoted again. To no one's surprise, the company's business struggled and in only a few years Frank left the company. I think most employees felt that perhaps many of the top field managers would have been far more successful had they had the chance to interview for the many jobs Frank was quickly passed through.

Leaders also can unfairly label employees and permanently eliminate them for consideration for promotion. I think it is clear that people constantly grow, learn, and change throughout life. Once labeled, an employee's career growth is frequently over. The president of one of the companies I worked with had a bad tendency to do this. I would introduce him to a new employee, and he would chat with them for five minutes or so, and then announce that the person was not cut out for management. Nothing would change his opinion of the employee. Needless to say this also helps create zombies. Why try if there is no hope?

The more successful companies with which I have worked try and apply some basic logic to promotions. Systems are in place to assure the right candidates are chosen, and up-to-date job descriptions that accurately spell out assigned responsibilities are available. All open positions are posted, and qualified employees are interviewed utilizing the same team-interview process utilized for new employees.

The team-interview process for promotions generally works as follows:
- The hiring manager posts the position and performs the initial interviews with internal and external candidates to winnow the list to three to five potential candidates.

- The hiring manager asks a minimum of three of his peers or superiors to conduct a second interview that the hiring manager will not attend. This team will interview potential candidates for the open position. If at all possible, these interviews should be arranged on the same day and be conducted by the same team. The interview and scoring process should take an hour to an hour and a half.

- The interview team will score the candidates in a variety of areas and then develop a final score and a 'hire' or 'no hire' recommendation.

- The hiring manager will make the most logical decision possible based on all the information available about the candidate including:

  - Knowledge of past performance. If this is a current employee, actual past performance has to carry the most weight. A one-hour interview should not take precedence over ten years of known performance.
  - The manager's personal interviews with the candidate.
  - The scores and recommendations from the team-interview process. If the team recommended not hiring the candidate, the hiring manager would need approval from the president or head of the division to make the hire.

This process accomplishes several objectives:
- Internal candidates who are not chosen feel that they were given fair consideration for the position.
- The team that interviewed and approved the candidate is now invested in the candidate's future success because they helped choose the candidate.

- If an external candidate is chosen, at least employees feel there is a fair system in place, and the new employee did not just show up "out of the blue."
- Requiring a senior executive's approval to hire an employee rejected by the team offers a final check to ensure that the most suitable candidates are hired.

When I have recommended that clients adopt such a system, I frequently hear that they just do not have the time. These same clients are frequently suffering from poor employee morale and high turnover. If they simply invested a little more time and effort into effective hiring and promotions, than they would not have to repeat the process nearly so often. Systems that are put in place to ensure fair treatment of employees are absolutely essential for generating a high level of energy within an organization. This is how organizations avoid zombies and nurture engaged and effective employees who enjoy their jobs.

I have been amazed by how often I find myself talking to a high-level Wal-Mart employee who started as a cashier. Based on input and ambition, anyone in Wal-Mart can be promoted. This helps keep everyone motivated.

Chapter 20
Honest Feedback and Performance Appraisals

Honest feedback can be divided into two areas:
- Communication to employees about what they are doing positively and communication about where they need to improve.
- Performance appraisals

Honest Feedback

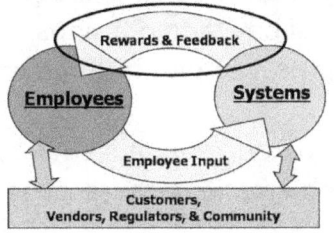

- It is unfair <u>not</u> to tell someone where they need to improve.

- Let them know you have confidence in them.

- Ask what they need to succeed. Ask what they think.

By now you have realized the importance I place on leaders recognizing and listening to their employees. I have heard many leaders say it does not make sense to recognize employees for simply doing their job, but I simply cannot understand that way of thinking. Employees work hard, and it never hurts to recognize their effort.

Some leaders constantly praise everyone and never address poor performance, and others rarely positively recognize anyone and are critical of everyone. In both cases, employees really do not know where they stand. I believe the right approach is to recognize and thank everyone for positive performance as much as humanly possible, while also clearly and honestly addressing areas where employees need to improve.

As a leader, I fell into the first category, and for the most part did not want to address controversial issues. The best way to handle employee problems frequently seemed to avoid addressing them. At one point in my career, I was told that if a poor review is a surprise to an employee, or if an employee is surprised when terminated for poor performance, then you have done a very poor job as a manager. Managers are doing their employees a *disservice* by not telling them where they need to improve, and employees deserve to be given every chance to improve.

We have already covered the day-to-day importance of honest positive feedback, but we should also address the formal, annual process of feedback that many organizations have in the form of performance appraisals. Because our environmental business unit was part of a very large and established company with a solid human resources infrastructure, an established performance appraisal system for all employees was in place when I took over. Performance appraisals were due annually for all employees and were a prerequisite before an employee could receive an annual pay raise or bonus. Like any system, there was always room for improvement, but at least a standardized system was in place.

One of the companies for which I worked required employee ratings to fit on a bell curve. That was problematic because it meant that a department of high-performing employees was forced to rank some low, some in the middle, and some high, and adjustments were frequently made after employee evaluations had been completed and submitted. A few weeks after an employee had received his evaluation, his manager might receive a call from senior management telling him to lower the employee's rating. You can imagine how well that helped the employee's morale.

Another problem with this company's performance reviews was that the job descriptions, pay ranges, and possible raises were set in stone to some degree. When the smoke cleared a really strong employee might receive a 4 percent raise, but a much weaker employee would receive a 2 percent raise. After taxes, there was not much reward based on a stronger performance. This type of a system forces good employees to leave and weaker employees to stay.

One of the mid-sized companies I worked for did not have much structure to their appraisal process, and their compensation system was somewhat chaotic. I talked to some employees who had been employed for fifteen years and had never had a performance appraisal. Many did not even know what their job title was, and pay ranges were all over the place. Again, this is a recipe for collecting an organization of zombies.

A final problem I have witnessed at many companies is that managers do not like to do performance appraisals, so they make appointments with their employees and then keep rescheduling. This is another huge morale killer. If a performance appraisal is postponed, most employees assume it is because they are going to receive a worse rating than expected. To be fair, systems need to be in place to ensure performance appraisals are conducted once a year and performance updates are conducted once a quarter, and appointments do appraisals are set in stone.

I have witnessed a considerable amount of frustration by employees and managers because employee appraisals are frequently outdated and do not reflect the company's current direction. Performance appraisals are the perfect forum to promote and measure employees

in terms of concepts such as the Employee Induction Motor. There are six primary sections within Employee Induction Motor:
- Input for improvement
- Recognition/feedback
- Do the right thing
- Engaged and effective employees who enjoy their job
- Ecstatic Customers
- Long-term profitability

I suggest that performance appraisals pose questions targeting each of the six areas. Questions might include:

Input for improvement:
- What ideas did you submit last year to help improve the effectiveness of the organization?
- Provide examples of input from fellow employees that you think helped them do their jobs better?
- Did you ensure that the concepts of the Employee Induction Motor were reviewed at the beginning of every meeting?

Recognition/feedback
- Who are the fellow employees you recognized last year? Whom did you recognize verbally, and whom did you recognize formally? For what did you recognize them?
- Are you a part of an Improvement Recognition and Communication committee? Have you contributed to an ICR committee?

Do the right thing
- What have you done to contribute to our high standards in the areas of:
    - Safety
    - Health
    - Regulatory compliance

- Positive community relations
- Protecting the environment

- Provide an example of an honest mistake you made last year. Tell us how you handled it, and what you learned from it.
- Provide an example of an honest mistake another employee made that may have affected you. How did you handle it?

Engaged and effective employees who enjoy their job
- What have you done to help yourself become more productive and increase your enjoyment of your job?
- How have you been a positive influence for your coworkers?
- What have you done to help your coworkers become more effective and enjoy their jobs more?
- Have you openly shared information with coworkers?
- Have you openly accepted input from coworkers?
- Have you accepted honest feedback from coworkers without taking it personally?
- Have you acted in a professional manner?
- Have you participated in any team interviews?
- Have all new employees gone through their initiation training?
- Have you assisted with initiation or management training?

Ecstatic customers
- How have you helped ensure customers are ecstatic about our products and services?
- If you do not have direct contact with customers, how have you helped coworkers ensure our customers are ecstatic about our products and services?
- Have you always shown empathy when a customer has a problem? (Showing empathy means you are not assessing who is at fault. It means that you are sincerely sorry that our customer is having a problem.)

- What have you done to track customer complaints and lost accounts? What system modifications have you recommended to help reduce these issues?

Long-term profitability
- How have you managed expenses for your job?
- Have you helped improve systems to help improve efficiency?
- Have you worked with vendors to help promote long-term positive relations that resulted in improved efficiencies for both parties?
- Have you helped improve systems, operations, or procedures to help ensure long-term profitability?

With each of these questions, goals should be established for the coming year. Two final questions should be included on all performance appraisals:
- What would you like to accomplish during your career, and what training and experience do you plan to acquire during the next year to move toward your goal?
- How can I help?

Chapter 21
Nonperforming Employees

As we discussed earlier, leadership is not royalty. It is also not the Mafia. Leaders cannot go around "whacking" people's careers for no good reason. While screaming "You're fired!" might make for an interesting television show, it does not work well within an organization. If everyone is walking around on pins and needles, worried about being fired, employees will quickly become zombies – careful to look busy but also careful not to rock the boat. Employees who are afraid to make waves inhibit innovation.

Improperly managing nonperforming employees is a weakness that I have witnessed at almost every company with which I have worked. During the nine years I managed our very successful environmental business inside of a chemical distribution company we fired and reprimanded very few employees. That's how I believe most businesses should operate. If the right people are hired and properly integrated into the organization and leaders are properly recognizing and rewarding employees while providing honest feedback, there should be no need for a constant cycle of hiring and firing. If that does happen, the leaders are at fault not the employees.

You cannot terminate someone's career for no good reason

While working for one company, I was forced to "whack" one of my employees for what seemed to me no legitimate reason. He was a manager who worked directly under me, and he was the first to give a speech about his facility as part of a new program that was intended to help senior management understand what was actually happening in the field. Because he was the first to speak, he was not sure what leadership wanted from his presentation. To make matters worse, he tended to sound arrogant when he spoke (although he was not) and he was not the most gifted public speaker.

This individual had built a regional facility from scratch; it was his baby, and he worked tirelessly to provide outstanding service to sales personnel and customers. His facility was very profitable and had perfect compliance. Nevertheless, without any warning, I was told to demote him and remove him from the facility because of that one bad presentation. I protested and was told if I did not follow orders, then I would be demoted. I did as I was told and watched this individual's career and even health severely deteriorate. I still feel sick about it today.

I was consulting for another company when the owner insisted that her sales manager terminate a salesperson without any justification. Reluctantly, the sales manager followed orders and released the individual on a Friday. On Monday, the owner of the company asked her sales manager to create and postdate reports to document this individual's poor performance. The very talented and highly qualified sales manager quit, and I also decided to end my relationship with the company. Leaders need to hold themselves accountable and lead by example. Respect for leadership depends on both what is said and, perhaps most importantly, what is done.

There are few secrets within an organization and everyone seems to know what is happening. No one should be above the company guidelines. In the above case, everyone in the company knew about this incident and morale was absolutely terrible. Within a year, this company was essentially closed, and the owners sold the customer list at a fire-sale price to their biggest competitor.

As the aforementioned examples illustrate, many of the companies with which I worked did not address nonperforming employees consistently or effectively. Managers and leaders tend to become frustrated with an employee and decide to terminate the individual - often without giving the individual any clue as to what needs to be done differently first. At one of the companies I worked with one of the human resources managers told me that far too often, managers would come to her and announce that they wanted an employee fired because he was not doing his job correctly. She would ask if the manager had ever told the employee that he was doing his job incorrectly, and the manager would respond, "No, I just want to fire him."

These managers had made a decision to fire the employee and just want to go through the motions until the unwanted employee is out the door. Frequently the manager does not want the employee to realize the seriousness of the situation; the manager wants to sneak up and fire the employee at the drop of a hat. That type of leadership is a recipe for poor morale. It reminds me of the movie *Animal House* (1978), when the dean placed a fraternity on "double secret probation." Without understanding the reasoning behind disciplinary action, it seems arbitrary, and employees will react like the fraternity members who continued to misbehave because they felt they were going to be expelled (or fired) no matter what they did. This is why it is so important to be honest with employees on an ongoing basis about their performance, and to always assume they can improve if given the chance.

I think there are several considerations managers should keep in mind when it comes to honestly providing feedback to employees:

- **Leaders need to take responsibility and realize that if they are constantly discussing poor performance and disciplinary procedures with employees, they have failed as leaders.** If this is happening, leaders are either making bad hiring decisions and failing to integrate people into their company, or they are doing a bad job of managing their overall operation. Most of the communication between managers and employees should be positive feedback for all of the good things employees have accomplished. Workers crave positive feedback so much that they should receive positive feedback perhaps 100 times more often than constructive or critical feedback.

- Just as leaders are being unfair to their employees if they do not explain how they need to improve, leaders are also being unfair if they give employees unrealistic reviews. Proper communication between managers and employees means a review rating will not be a surprise to an employee

- If disciplinary measures are handled fairly and understood by all employees, the morale of the whole team will actually improve. It is very frustrating for the best workers to watch poor workers continue in their position without any input from management. If employees who have been clearly told how to improve fail to improve, or if employee's actions are egregious, it is essential that fair and formal disciplinary procedures are taken.

We utilized a tiered approach to non-performing employees in our environmental organization within the chemical distribution company. One aspect was somewhat unique at the time- in all cases there was an opportunity for the disciplined employee to clear his record. The steps were as follows:

- Documented Verbal warning – These are generally used for less serious problems where the employee's need for improvement has been regularly discussed with the employee. For this level of discipline, the employee is told that they are being issued a formal verbal warning and that it will be documented in his employee record. The employee is told specifically what is required of him in the future. If the employee has no further issues requiring formal discipline for six months, the verbal warning documentation will be removed from his employee record and destroyed.

- Written warning – These are generally used when an employee has been given a verbal warning, and he fails to meet the requirements stated in the verbal warning. These warnings will clearly spell out where the employee needs to improve, and the employee will be asked to sign the document. The written document will contain language warning the employee that continued poor performance will result in further discipline. Again, like any warning, these can be issued even if the performance situation has not been previously discussed if the situation is egregious. If the employee has no further issues for a year, the written warning documentation will be removed from his employee record and destroyed.

- Decision Making Leave – This is a one-day suspension with pay intended to give the employee the opportunity to decide if he wants to be a team player and a productive employee of the company. Again, these warnings will clearly spell out where the employee needs to improve, and the employee will be asked to sign the document. The written document will contain language warning the employee that continued poor performance will result in further discipline that can include termination. Documentation of these warnings will remain in the employee's file for two years assuming there are no further problems requiring discipline.

- Paid suspension pending investigation – This is used when an employee is investigated for situations like theft, blatant disregard of safety, or regulatory requirements. As soon as the investigation is concluded, the employee will either be exonerated or receive one of the formal disciplinary actions described above or even termination as described below.

- Termination – Generally all terminations will be preceded by the previous disciplinary actions, but some egregious acts such as theft, threatening another employee, or blatant disregard for regulations may result in immediate termination. For some reason employees frequently believe they are always entitled to two weeks of pay after termination, however for severe situations an immediate dismissal is supported by most state laws and pay can be terminated immediately.

In order to maintain fairness and consistency, policies need to ensure that key personnel such as a manager's supervisor and human resources participate in disciplinary decisions. Decision Making

Leaves, terminations, and suspensions pending investigation need to be approved by senior management.

Perhaps this seems to be an odd topic for a book on employee motivation, but it strikes me as essential. An organization without rules for discipline that are understood by all employees would be like a football game without standardized and understood penalties. If the referee had no guidelines and a holding penalty was sometimes a three yard penalty and other times thirty yards, the game would be chaos and the players would be highly frustrated. The discipline program we utilized within our environmental business unit was actually a morale builder because everyone understood the rules and it was implemented fairly. Every employee likes to know where he or she stands.

American Business in a Global Economy

Chapter 22
What Has Changed in the United States?

I wrote this final section to facilitate some discussion on how business leadership in the United States may share some responsibility for our difficult economy. This section is based upon my thoughts and observations as well as hard data from the U.S. Bureau of Labor and Statistics.

The transition began around 1980 when our country's business culture seemed to change as leadership began to shift toward making money in the short-term as opposed to focusing on the long-term success of their entire business entity. Because long-term strategies do not produce immediate returns, many CEOs and company leaders began to gravitate toward a strategy of vast reorganizing and restructuring to boost, or at least appear to be trying to boost, short-term performance. In many cases these same leaders paid themselves handsomely for their efforts to create change, even before any positive return was generated.

When I recall the relationships I had with hundreds of companies before the late 1980s, I am struck by the absence of employees who were upset by continual reorganizations and restructuring. However, since 1990, almost everyone I talk with from many different organizations is most frustrated by continual reorganizations and restructuring. It is as if U.S. business leadership has headed toward incredibly short-term thinking and is fixated on the notion of "How can I do something quickly and dramatically to demonstrate to shareholders, the board, customers, concerned citizens, and employees that I am taking action?" Unfortunately for everyone involved, the answer often is to continually restructure and reorganize, just as my second employer did repeatedly when the chemical waste industry slowed down.

While our country's shift to ultra short-term thinking seems to be ineffectual for many organizations, statistics seem to indicate it is particularly damaging to manufacturing and other industries that require long-term investments and strategies. The United States has lost a huge number of manufacturing jobs since 1979. Per the Bureau of Labor and Statistics (BLS) (2009), manufacturing jobs have decreased from a peak of 19,426,000 at the end of 1979 to 11,986,000 as of May 2009. As the following chart demonstrates, the pace of manufacturing job losses has accelerated dramatically since 2000 with 5,277,000 lost between December 2000 and May 2009. These losses cannot simply be blamed on the severe recession of late 2008 because most of these losses occurred before the recession began.

U.S. Manufacturing Jobs since WWII
Per the U.S. Bureau of Labor and Statistics (1,000's)

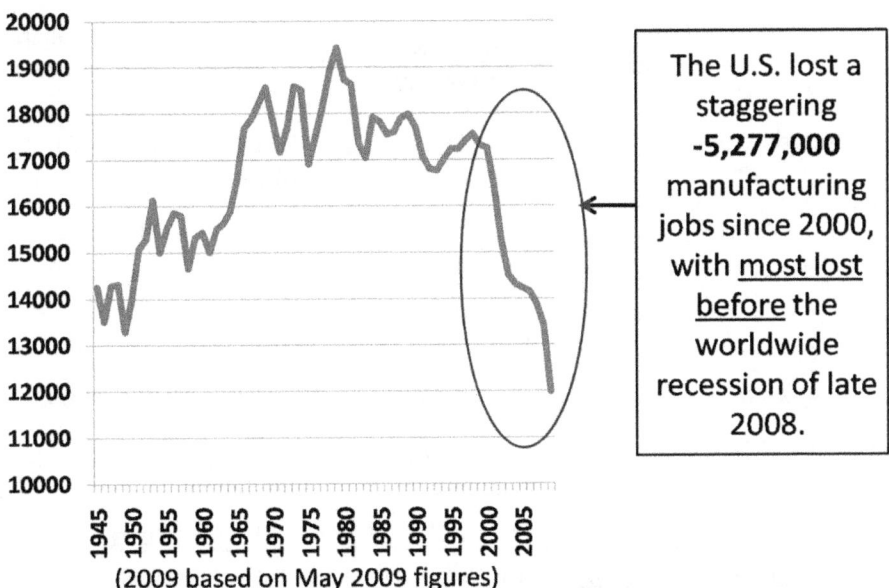

(2009 based on May 2009 figures)

The U.S. lost a staggering **-5,277,000** manufacturing jobs since 2000, with <u>most lost before</u> the worldwide recession of late 2008.

    The common perception is that the loss of manufacturing jobs in the United States is due to increased efficiency requiring fewer workers, coupled with a shift to purchase more products from countries with less regulations and lower wages such as China. For these reasons, shifting toward a service-oriented United States job base seems like a natural transition. I was curious how manufacturing jobs in the United States have been affected in contrast to countries with similar regulations and wages.

    The following chart, created using information available from the BLS, compares the United States to six similar countries from 1998 to 2007.

Comparison to Countries with Similar Wages and Regulations
(Data from the Bureau of Labor and Statistics)

	Mfg. Jobs Lost 1998-2007	Percent of Mfg. Jobs Lost 1998-2007	Mfg. Jobs as a Percent of 2007 Civilian Workforce	2007 Civilian Workforce
United States	**-4,431,000**	**-21.4%**	**11.2%**	**146,047,000**
Japan	-2,160,000	-15.7%	18.3%	63,510,000
Germany	-296,000	-3.4%	22.2%	37,815,000
Sweden	-112,000	-14.5%	14.6%	4,530,000
Italy	-89,000	-1.8%	21.2%	22,953,000
Canada	-48,000	-2.3%	12.2%	16,767,000
Netherlands	-21,000	-1.8%	13.2%	8,408,000
Excluding the United States	-2,726,000	-9.5%	18.6%	153,983,000

The <u>**United States lost 1,705,000 (62.5%) more manufacturing jobs**</u> than all of these countries combined!

If manufacturing jobs are the core of a healthy economy, the story this chart reveals is frightening. From 1998-2007 all of these countries also lost manufacturing jobs most likely due to increased efficiencies and the purchase of more products from countries like China; however the United States lost 1,705,000, or 62.5 percent more manufacturing jobs than *all* of these countries combined! In 2007 all of these countries employed a greater percent of their workforce in manufacturing than the United States. During this ten year period these other countries lost an average of 9.5 percent of their manufacturing jobs compared to 21.4 percent for the United States. In 2007 manufacturing jobs for these other six countries combined averaged 18.6 percent of their total workforce compared to only 11.2 percent for the United States.

According to the BLS the United States lost an additional 1,440,000 more manufacturing jobs since this study was completed (as of May 2009), and as a percent of the total workforce manufacturing jobs are now at the lowest level since the beginning of the industrial revolution. This large loss in manufacturing jobs compared to these other countries indicates that something is amiss in United States that was not before 1979, and it is up to us to correct this problem before it has even more negative consequences.

Historically manufacturing jobs have been important for several reasons. First, manufacturing jobs provide products to sell to other countries, which helps to maintain a healthy national trade balance. Second, the large investment required for manufacturing generally provides for more long-term sustainable employment compared to many service sector jobs. Third, because manufacturing jobs create more value by actually building a product to sell, manufacturing companies can afford to pay for more health care and other benefits. Finally, manufacturing capacity has historically proven to be important for defense to quickly build newly required military equipment without relying on imports.

It is no coincidence that the balance of trade for the United States aligns almost perfectly with the chart tracking manufacturing jobs since WWII. Prior to 1979 our country maintained a trade balance without large deficits or surpluses. After 1979 the United States began to generate ever-increasing trade deficits that grew to a massive $763 billion annually by 2006 (US Census, 2007). It may be no coincidence that Americans have steadily lost health care and other benefits during this period because manufacturing jobs create more value than service jobs, thus allowing employers to offer better benefits. Also as manufacturing jobs disappear and health care jobs increase with an aging population, many employees have shifted from manufacturing to service jobs in the health care industry, further increasing our health care costs without creating any value to pay for it.

Trade suffers with less to sell to other countries and employee benefits are reduced because little real value is being created in the U.S.

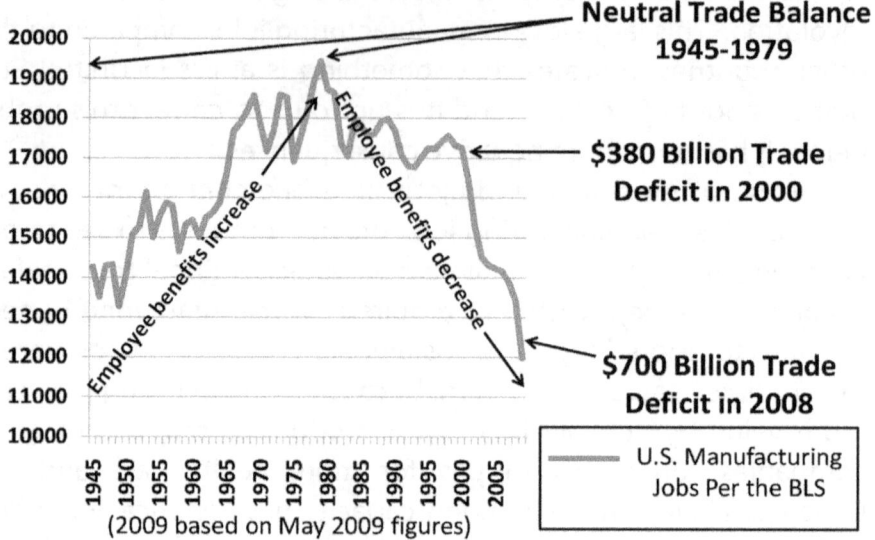

(2009 based on May 2009 figures)

If the United States continues to lose 5.3 million manufacturing jobs per decade, then in twenty years manufacturing jobs will be virtually nonexistent, and at some point we will no longer be an industrialized nation. One has to wonder if we can continue to maintain our world superpower status with minimal manufacturing capacity.

No one knows all of the contributing factors for why the United States is losing manufacturing jobs at such a fast rate, but I believe several key areas are involved with these losses:

- In the 1980's it became a popular notion that it was good for Americans to become rich as quickly as possible, creating a business culture seeking quick financial gains at the expense of creating any long-term value for the organization. This has forced business leadership to create short-term and top-down strategies with little time for input from employees.

- Because one of the quickest returns is in the financial community, many talented individuals have chosen a financial career path instead of industries like manufacturing. The increased focus on "getting rich quick" has caused the financial community to shift from providing long-term loans for manufacturing and other industries that create real value for our country, to an industry driven by risky trading, unregulated financial instruments few understand, and consumer loans often with extortion like interest rates. Instead of supporting industry the financial community has become its own entity unrelated to the rest of the economy.

The proof of this can be seen in 2009 where risky behavior seemed to be encouraged and rewarded. If the market crashes as it did in early 2009 this actually benefits the financial community because the market can then be manipulated to dramatically increase allowing huge profits again for financial companies and employees. For the Dow Jones Industrial Average to increase by 50% from its low of 6,500 in March to over 10,000 in October, while the national unemployment rate remained near ten percent and major industries including housing, manufacturing, and the auto industry were still in shambles, demonstrates today's complete disconnect between the financial community and our nation's industry. It certainly appears that individuals in the financial community are chasing fast personal wealth. In October 2009, while most of the country was still suffering, JP Morgan, Goldman Sachs, and Citibank recorded massive profits, paying employees huge bonuses. For 2009 Goldman Sachs combined bonuses and salaries averaged $700,000 for every employee in their organization.

- Because the financial community is focused on quick returns from trading, derivative markets, and consumer loans, there is little interest in investing in industries like manufacturing that create value. This desire for quick returns from industry limits investments in new equipment and robotics. The huge gains in manufacturing efficiency due to computerization and robotics have actually allowed countries with higher labor costs to compete in the manufacturing of higher quality and more expensive products. Unfortunately our focus towards a quick return severely limits business leaders' ability to invest in the new equipment required. Business leaders are forced to promote short-term strategies to restructure because there is little interest in any real investment in their business.

- CEO assignments are becoming short-term with the goal of a quick turn-around and large personal gains for themselves, further eliminating the option of investing in long-term manufacturing strategies. While this trend has not helped critical industries like manufacturing, it has dramatically increased CEO compensation. Our CEOs now make ten times as much as their Japanese peers and three times more than European CEOs (Moberg, 2009).

- The trend toward restructuring for short-term gains encourages shipping manufacturing jobs overseas. CEOs can point to their strategy by simply saying, "Look at how we have reduced costs by eliminating jobs," and investors react positively. While Wall Street receives a short-term "high" when stocks are boosted after lay-offs are announced, our country suffers when these jobs represent actual manufacturing capacity. Imports increase, exports decrease, and our base of tax payers shrink. The following chart from the September 21, 2009 copy of Business Week demonstrates how manufacturing capacity is shrinking relative to economic growth. Because real value was not being created, perhaps this explains the severity of the recession that followed.

Manufacturing Capacity Compared to Economic Growth

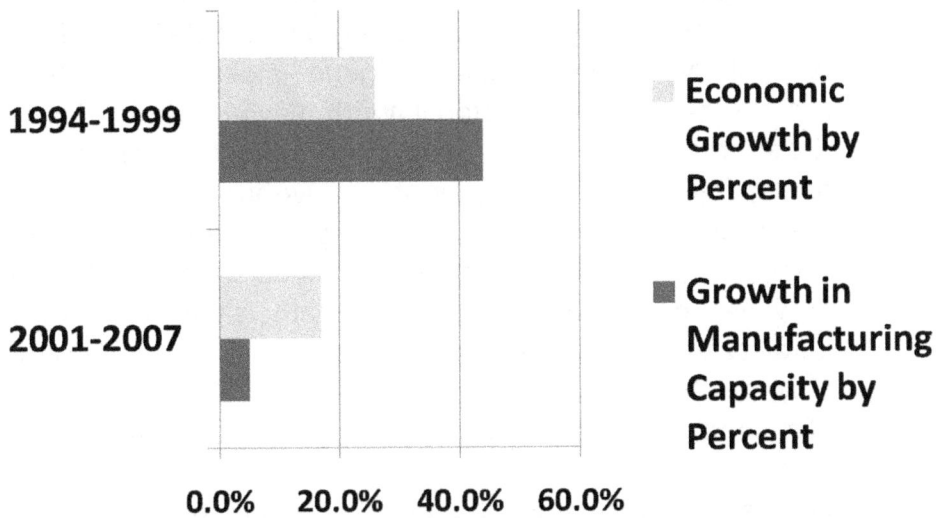

Business Week, Sept 21, 2009 - Analysis by James C. Cooper
Data: Federal Reserve Bank

- There are few government incentives to keep manufacturing jobs in the United States. Recently organizations were actually given tax breaks to ship jobs overseas (U.S. Government Accountability Office, 2005). Manufacturing jobs should not have to be artificially supported to stay in the United States; however they should also not be artificially supported to leave.

- From an educational perspective, our country is perhaps overly focused on traditional scholastic capabilities of students. The current perception in the United States is that the only acceptable job route is to go to college, get a white collar job, and try and make as much money as possible as quickly as possible. Historically, students that were not strong in traditional scholastic intelligence gravitated toward manufacturing jobs.

Many other countries test for these skills and provide vocational training, since these types of students frequently have different strengths, including mechanical or hands-on intelligence. There is even research that suggests some students actually struggle at reading because their very high level of three-dimensional intelligence makes it difficult to process the two dimensional written word (Davis, 1994). Other students do not do well in school because they tend to daydream about all kinds of creative ideas. Historically, these students could frequently become great innovators. Today these students are often dismissed as failures before they even get a chance to start their careers because of their inability to pass standardized testing. If the goal is to send everyone to college to obtain a job sitting in a cubicle in front of a computer, who is going to actually assemble anything?

On the contrary, many of the brightest students as measured by to scholastic intelligence may have little or no experience with hands-on intelligence. This point was recently driven home when I was watching a local program called the Brain Game, where the most intelligent kids from local high schools compete by answering very difficult questions about history, math, and science, among other topics. In one round, the subject turned to woodworking and the first question was, "What do you call a machine that spins a piece of wood where you put a chisel against the wood to carve the wood symmetrically?" The students from both teams stared blankly at the host and were unable to answer. The next question was, "What do you call a device that has a blade and two handles that you slide along a piece of wood to shave off a thin layer?" Again, all the contestants had blank expressions and no answer (Wright, 2007). It is clear these very bright students had no idea what a lathe or a plane was and have possibly never even touched a raw piece of wood.

What Has Changed in the United States?

It is perhaps this one size fits all educational philosophy that has caused such a high rate of unemployment for workers under 24 in the United States. According to an article titled The Lost Generation in Business Week's October 2009 issue, the United States unemployment rate for workers under 24 is 18.2% versus 10.8% for Germany and 9.3% for Japan (Coy, 2009).

- Perhaps all of these factors have caused most Americans to simply accept the idea that it is a "natural progression" for the United States to gravitate toward a service-based economy, so the loss of manufacturing jobs is a self-fulfilling prophecy.

Whatever the reasons, it seems like business leaders in the United States have become a nation of short-term thinkers who restructure and reorganize so often that our workforce now includes a huge number of zombie employees sitting in cubicles. Many years ago, Peter Drucker (1954), the godfather of modern management philosophy, warned about the *activity trap* where there is a lot of activity with little actual contribution. In many ways our nation has fallen into one giant activity trap.

Recently, I was giving a presentation on the subject of the lost U.S. manufacturing jobs, and a participant asked if I had read General Electric's annual letter to its shareholders from GE CEO Jeffery Immelt. I had not; however, as soon as I was back in my office I pulled up the letter dated February 6, 2009. Immelt is clearly thinking along the same lines as myself. His comments are as follows:

> "I have also learned something about my country. I run a global company, but I am a citizen of the U.S. I believe a popular 30 year notion that the U.S. can evolve from a technology and a manufacturing leader to a service leader is just wrong. In the end, this philosophy transformed the financial services

industry from one that supported commerce to a complex trading market that operated outside of the economy. Real engineering was traded for financial engineering. In the end, our business, our government, and many local leaders lost sight of what makes a nation great: a passion for innovation.

To this end, we need an education system that inspires hard work, discipline, and creative thinking. The ability to innovate must be valued again. We must discover new technologies and develop a productive manufacturing base. Our trade deficit is a sign of real weakness and we must reduce our debt to the world." (Immelt, 2009)

If we could shift toward a leadership style that could harness the energy of all employees and convert the zombies into a productive and innovative workforce that is actually producing something, I cannot imagine how we would not dramatically increase the productivity of all jobs, including those in manufacturing.

The zombie factor may be further enhanced in the United States because so many organizations no longer offer health care and benefits. Not long ago, quitting a job because of frustration with the direction of company leaders was less of a concern than it is today. Most companies offered benefits, and employees would be covered when they moved to a new job. I know many employees who absolutely hate their jobs but stay on with a company because they are too afraid to lose benefits. It almost harkens back to the days when employees owed their soul to the company store. Even though Canada's nationalized health care system is far from perfect, business leaders in Canada have told me that they are well aware that if they continually make bone-headed decisions, employees will simply go elsewhere, knowing they will still have basic health care.

The television program *Archie Bunker* was so funny in the early 1970s because it pointed out the irrationality of bigotry that was common at that time. The reason the sitcom *The Office* is so popular today is that it highlights the absurdity of much of the current organizational leadership in this country. This is not to say that everyone in 1970 was a bigot or that every leader today is leading an organization of zombies. There are plenty of good leaders and organizations out there, but like the bigotry of the 1970s, there are so many companies caught in Drucker's activity trap today that it is a common joke among employees.

Chapter 23
What Has Changed in Today's Global Economy?

Information management and distribution is changing at a blindingly fast pace, due mainly to the extremely rapid advancement of innovations in computer technology and networking. This has increased global competition because of the resulting changes to how both buyers and sellers operate. Because of this new networking technology, buyers are now better able to find the best options available while sellers can integrate new technology into their organization to improve their systems and capabilities.

Used here, the term *sellers* refers to manufacturing, retail, service, or any business organizations that must sell products or services to buyers in order to be successful.

Information distribution through networking and computers has had such a dramatic affect on the world that I am not sure any of us can fully comprehend it. In 1985, I was branch manager for a chemical distribution facility in western, New York. I was running a $16 million business that included a warehouse, tank farm, sales team, customer service team, and a team of driver/warehouseman personnel. To provide any special pricing to customers, I needed approval from my regional manager at corporate. In addition to myself, my regional manager was also responsible for five additional branch managers

What has <u>changed</u> in today's global business environment for <u>all</u> organizations?

- <u>Buyers</u> have immediate access anywhere in the world to find the best:
  - Vendors.
  - Products & services.
  - Pricing and benefits.
  - Transportation costs.

- <u>Sellers</u> integrate new computing & global information capabilities into their organization:
  - Improve efficiencies within their organization.
  - Improve the quality of products and services manufactured and delivered.
  - Interact directly with customers, vendors, and others via systems as well as employees.

Sellers include anyone in business to manufacture or distribute a product or service for sale.

who were my peers. Each of my peers was also responsible for a facility and area around a large city such as Cleveland, Pittsburgh, and Akron. My regional manager would not reveal to me the competitive truckload price for a given chemical in Cleveland because that was a completely different market despite being a mere three hours from my western New York facility. Cleveland might have a lower truckload price and it might take six months or more before it spread to our market. Even though the branch manager in Cleveland was one of my closest friends in the company, when we talked we did not share special deals we had in our market for fear of leaks that would lower someone else's market.

The same concept held true when we sold chemicals to national accounts with many locations. Even though they were all part of one company, we would frequently deliver chemicals to each location at a different price based on what the local market would allow. After all, nobody at that time utilized a nationwide computing system, and even if they did, they were afraid that communicating their secret price to a sister location might ruin their special deal. Even the name of the department was significant, since the majority of the clients operated exclusively within the United States it was called the National Accounts Department's. The department was later changed to the Corporate Accounts Department as we gradually started selling to companies with corporate headquarters outside the United States.

One of our strong selling points in 1985 was that we only carried American made chemicals. This was not because we were particularly patriotic—it was mostly due to the fact that imported chemicals generally came through brokers with little control over product quality and assurance of continuous supply.

Even though our western New York operation was over $15 million in sales with nearly twenty employees, we did not have a single computer or terminal of any kind at our facility in 1985. All orders were typed and batches of typed invoices were mailed to corporate, where the data was entered into computers to generate invoices and corporate records. The only process improvements came from our implementation of a new form or procedure. The only competition we experienced was from a handful of local competitors.

How the world has changed! Now we can research and order products from China and other parts of the world in seconds, and the quality and consistency of supplies are forever improving. In many ways, China feels closer today than Cleveland did in 1985! Today, most companies face many new competitors through the Internet, and the pace of process improvements has dramatically increased because of new computer technology.

Chapter 24
What Has Not Changed?

The good news for everyone who sells products and services is that one aspect has not changed—customers still buy from organizations they like (or love) best for a variety of reasons beyond price.

What has <u>not</u> changed?

- **Customers still buy from *<u>organizations</u>* they like (or love) best, for a variety of reasons, besides simply the price.**

- **(Brand Loyalty)**

　　Let us take a look at some organizations that have experienced more success recently than many of their competitors:

A look at some successful organizations customers like or love better than some competitors

- Southwest Airlines
- Amazon
- Best Buy
- Wegmans Grocery Stores

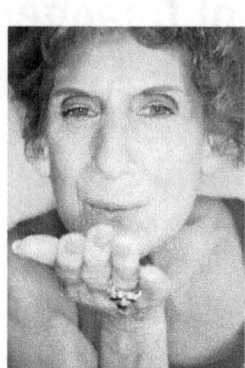

- Wal-Mart
- Target
- Honda
- Toyota

If you ask customers of these organizations why they buy from them, they will provide many reasons why they like, or even love, these organizations. You may not be familiar with Wegman's grocers, an upscale grocery chain in the Northeast that is doing very well and unlike other grocers isn't being hurt as severely by big box stores that now sell groceries. Once when I mentioned Wegman's at a presentation far from the Northeast an attendee enthusiastically added, "Wegman's is an amazing experience!" Other people who had never been to Wegman's looked at him like he was crazy; how could a grocery store be an amazing experience? If you talk with Wegman's customers, they almost always provide many reasons they love Wegman's stores. I was talking about Wegman's with my cousin, who lives in the Northeast, and he said, "But you don't understand. Nobody treats their employees better than Wegman's." He said it as if it was some kind of unfair advantage to treat your employees extremely well. It is no coincidence that Wegman's is always listed as one of the nation's top five employers to work for according to Fortune Magazine.

My wife and many of her friends will tell you why they absolutely love Target. I have friends who became disenchanted with traditional car companies' quality in the 1970s but are still in love with their Hondas or Toyotas. Instead of zombies, Wegman's and others on the above list of successful companies are full of engaged employees. An engaged employee is the opposite of a zombie but just as contagious.

"Engaged" employees
Enjoys what they do for a living because they are:

- Doing something productive

- Their input counts

- They are recognized and fairly rewarded

- Communicate openly and professionally including listening to input from others without being defensive

- Part of a work family were everyone takes responsibility and tries to "do the right thing"

I have yet to talk with a Southwest employee who does not enjoy working for the company, and although some people may not admit to enjoying shopping at Wal-Mart, their parking lots are always packed with loyal customers. Wal-Mart has combined systems and employees to provide excellent prices with quality merchandise.

The definition of brand loyalty is one idea that remains constant. Brand loyalty is all about how much customers like or love an organization. Organizations may offer unique products and services customers may buy short-term, but to remain viable long term, customers must like (hopefully love) the organization that produces and sells the products or services. The actual products Wegman's sells are mostly the same as their competitors; it is their organization that customers love.

Have you had a friend or relative who tried to fall in love with someone who was generally unhappy with himself, had no good system to effectively manage his life, was extremely greedy and thought only of his own personal greed, or was dishonest or unethical? It may work out for a while, but eventually the relationship falls apart. The same holds true for customers when they buy from organizations with these traits. It may work for the short term, but it's not going to last.

It is hard to fall "in love" with an individual or <u>organization</u> experiencing many of these issues:

- Generally unhappy with themselves.

- Full of strife and conflict.

- Have no good system to effectively manage themselves or their business.

- They are extremely greedy and only think of their own personal greed above all else.

- They are dishonest or unethical.

What Has Not Changed?

The dilemma organizations face today is that increased global competition and regulations coupled with constant restructuring can create increased pressures that reduce employee morale and effectiveness. As this happens, leaders tend to make even more dramatic decisions, further frustrating the organization, and more customers become unsatisfied and fall "out of love" with the organization. This in turn creates more pressure on the organization and the downward spiral continues.

I have talked to many industry leaders who tell me, "You don't understand. Our industry is ultra competitive, and there is no way to differentiate ourselves." Or "You don't understand. There are no good workers left." These leaders need to look at Honda and Toyota, who have built factories in the United States and are very successfully building world-class cars that compete anywhere using American workers. The difference is not the worker - it is the leadership.

Chapter 25
Traditional Leadership

In 1985, when I was managing a distribution facility, organizational leaders generally grew up within an organization. Because these leaders knew how the business operated, they came up with most of the ideas about how to run their business. Leaders would tell their organization what they decided to do, and workers followed suit. This made sense because most leaders were ambitious and relatively smart. As long as the organization was better than, or at least as good as, its local competition, the organization would be okay. Even companies that operated nationally only needed to worry about being as good as the competitors within the country. Now, due to the enormous gains in information management and distribution, everyone's competitive markets have greatly expanded; local markets have now become national, and national markets have become global.

Traditional leadership works much as the first internal combustion engines did. An organization's leaders made most of the decisions and pushed them down on their employees. Employees then interacted with customers and vendors, and the feeling was that the less anyone from the outside knew about what was going on inside the company, the better. Like early combustion motors, the idea was to generate power in terms of money, and no one was concerned with pollution or inefficiencies as long as the organization was profitable. Everyone knew who their boss was, and if you had a good boss then things were pretty good. The general structure of the organization was pretty stable. In this environment, leaders who made quick decisions were admired and promoted. Many times during this era I heard people say, "Make a decision, even if it is wrong."

Traditional Leadership
- Top down with fairly consistent leadership
- Some input from employees
- Employees generally understood and bought into new strategies and decisions being implemented
- Changes are not very dramatic or frequent

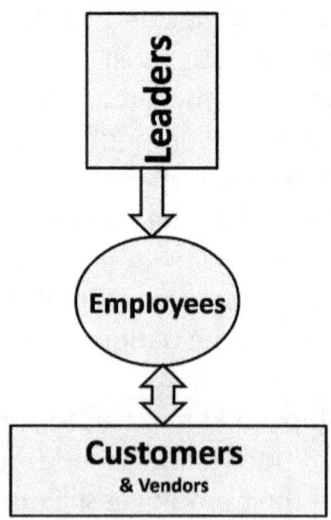

Traditional Leadership
(One cylinder combustion motor)

In the era of traditional leadership, leaders considered themselves a little bit like royalty. This seemed especially true when I worked at the chemical distribution company. Corporate headquarters was a series of beautiful chrome and glass buildings that were immaculately landscaped. There was an executive dining room on the top floor, giving the impression that executives did not want to associate with the "common folk."

Working in the field was much like being one of the peasants, since it seemed they spent as little money as possible operating and maintaining those facilities. It was the job of those in the field to make money utilizing what little assets corporate allowed. Frequently, our trucks were ancient and the facilities were dilapidated.

At this time, doing the right thing was often pretty far down on everyone's list. I started working for the chemical distribution company in the late 1970's. Amazingly enough, before 1980 there were no standardized laws regarding disposal of chemical waste. The standard practice for most companies was to pour it on the ground, pour it into the nearest waterway, or belch it into the sky. When I was growing up, every city had its own smell based on what was being manufactured nearby. On June 22, 1969, the Cuyahoga River in Cleveland, Ohio, actually caught fire because of the level of pollution in the water (Ohio History Central, 2009). The first chemical distribution facility at which I worked was in a small town and had earthen dikes surrounding the tank farm. The only person to inspect the facility was the fire marshal, who threatened to issue a violation if weeds grew on the dike. To avoid receiving a violation, the practice at the facility was to pour the spent chemicals used to rinse the delivery pipes over the dikes to kill the weeds. This practice was perfectly legal and no one thought anything of it at the time. Although the facility has been closed for twenty years, I assume the site is still contaminated.

In the days of traditional management, cheating was sometimes almost considered an art form. Often the idea was to get the job done even if it meant shorting a customer or not abiding by required regulations. Recently, I was reading about stock car racing, and a famous driver was quoted that in the early days, whoever could cheat the most and not get caught would win the most races (Jensen, 2002). Those days are over. Today stock cars are built to strict standards, and the winners are the teams that work the best within specific, strict regulations. I think in the next century the same will hold true for organizations. Organizations will need to abide by and work with regulations, and compliance will be built into the organizational structure.

Traditional Leadership under Increased Pressure

Eventually traditional leadership began to feel increased pressure from various outside influences. In the 1960s and 1970s, employee safety became a bigger issue, and during the 1970s and 1980s, environmental regulations began to emerge. The 1990s brought increased global competition, while the new information age allowed shareholders to measure and seek stocks with the quickest returns, giving investors very high, short-term expectations. In the 2000s, financial disclosure became an issue, and throughout all these years community activism might arise at any time.

As each new regulation was implemented, leaders insisted that the new requirements would put them out of business. Thus began the cry for deregulation or a return to the "good old days," when organizations could do whatever they wanted. I remember when fluorocarbons were first banned because of the problems with the ozone layer. I believe I heard from everyone in the industry that these chemicals were irreplaceable for air-conditioning and other uses, and yet new chemicals were quickly developed to replace them.

Traditional Leadership began to face new competition and more outside influences

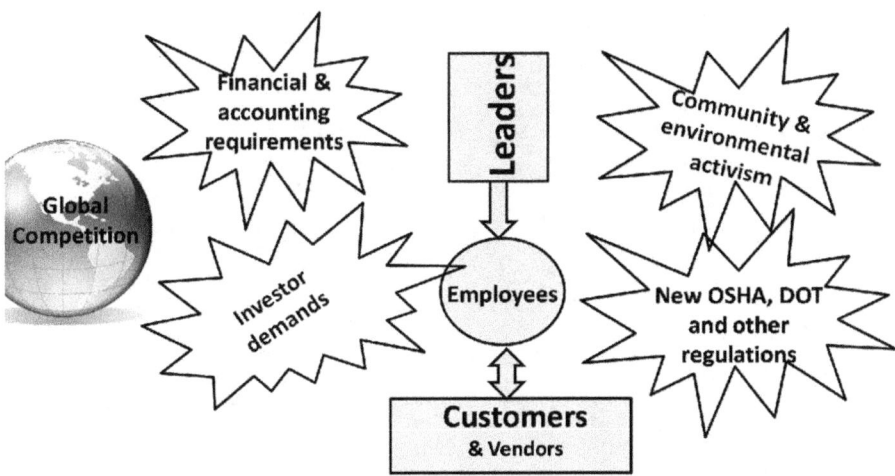

Under all this new pressure, traditional management had to do something. In the new information age, company decisions and strategies are broadcast to everyone. Staying the course and not at least giving the *appearance* of dramatic action was not well received. In the late 1980s traditional U.S. leadership began to transition to a faster paced style of leadership that was based on constant restructuring and reorganizing.

Chapter 26
Restructuring to Restructure Leadership

Sometime around the late 1980s to the early 1990s, this new short-term restructuring and reorganizing leadership style began to develop as it was utilized by leadership to demonstrate that they were dealing with the new competition and other outside influences. I call this *Restructuring to Restructure* leadership; however it could also be called *change for the sake of change* leadership. Frequently the changes are dramatic, with many different alterations being implemented at one time. Leaders cross their fingers and hope that they will somehow get lucky with all of the changes being implemented.

Restructuring to Restructure Leadership
- Top down generally with frequent leadership changes
- Often little or no input from employees
- Employees generally do not understand or buy into new strategies and decisions being implemented
- Dramatic and often frequent changes

"Restructuring to Restructure" Leadership

Multi-cylinder, high octane, turbo-charged, with everything changing at once. This causes a tremendous amount of wasted organizational energy!

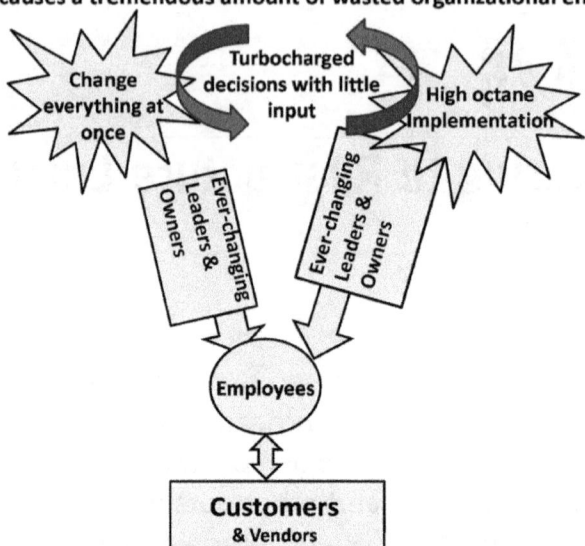

One of the results of the new Restructuring to Restructure leadership is a tremendous increase of wasted energy because the restructuring itself uses up much of an organizations' energy while also causing a high degree of burnout and dissatisfaction in employees. Restructuring to Restructure leadership frequently adds multiple cylinders of change that pound down on employees at a rapid pace, with turbo-charged decisions and high-octane implementation. I have spoken with many friends who roll their eyes and joke about the latest round of restructuring or reorganization at their company. Some organizations suffer reorganizations and restructuring multiple times in the same year.

The worst part of most Restructuring to Restructure leadership is that it frequently does not address many of the outside influences and increased global competition. It actually can make the problem worse by sapping energy from the organization. The Restructuring to Restructure model looks like mass chaos once all the outside influences and increased global competition are added.

"Restructuring to Restructure" Leadership
Also has to deal with even more outside influences and more global competition!

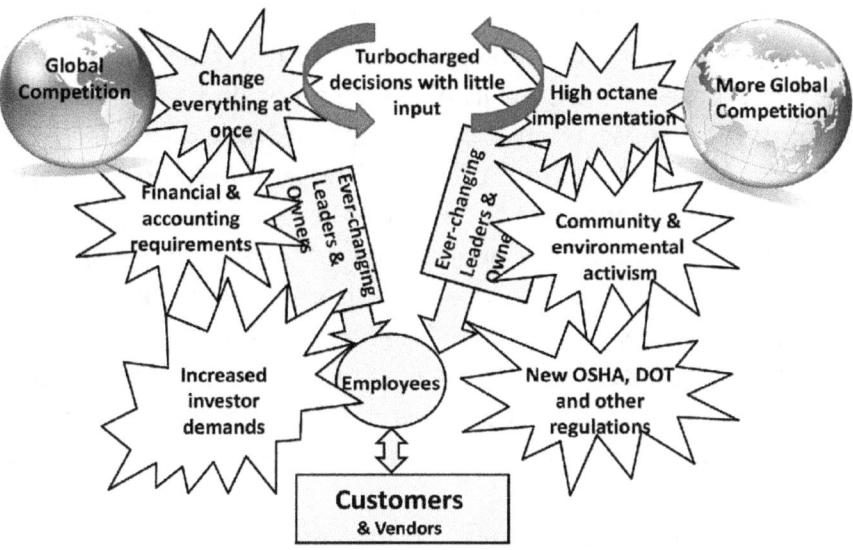

In 2008 and 2009, Pepsico was going through a cycle of what I would call Restructuring to Restructure leadership. According to *Business Week* (Holm, 2009), the plan called for "not just devising new ads and slogans for seven separate brands, but redesigning 1,121 different bottles, cans, and other packages." This was to be accomplished in seven months, which left no time to check consumer reaction to the changes. The new design for Tropicana had to be reversed almost immediately because of poor reception to the new package design by consumers. It remains to be seen how successful Pepsico's new strategy will be, however it is obviously risky to push so many changes rapidly down through an organization. *Business Week*'s title for the article about Pepsico's new plan was telling: "Blowing up Pepsi," and the subtitle read "Creative destruction - or just destruction?"

My first introduction to Restructuring to Restructure leadership occurred while I was working at the chemical distribution company. We had just successfully implemented our new leadership model within our environmental business unit to become one of the most profitable, compliant, and fastest-growing environmental businesses in the country. Although we were part of the chemical distribution company, we were operating autonomously, mostly because our business ran on an entirely separate set of regulations. About this time, the company brought in all new senior managers to run the distribution business, even though none of them had ever worked in the chemical distribution industry. These managers developed a plan to change everything at one time regardless of how well any methods were currently working. To confirm that the proposed changes were the correct course of action, these new leaders hired a very high-priced consulting firm. The firm was full of young graduate students who possessed little real world experience and together with our new leaders, concocted a plan to make many sweeping simultaneous changes throughout the entire chemical distribution company.

Before senior management's proposed changes, the company consisted of seventy facilities each with a warehouse and a tank farm. Each facility was responsible for a region of the country, and a branch manager who had full profit and loss responsibilities ran all aspects of each facility. It was very easy to determine and address profitability and revenue issues. The only recent exceptions to this model were the food grade chemical business unit and our environmental business, which happened to be two of the newer and faster growing business units. Both businesses were so heavily regulated and the required knowledge so specific that we very successfully built separate organizations and facilities within the company. Most of the branch managers were thrilled we were operating separately because the burden of the regulations associated with our two businesses made it almost impossible for them to operate their primary business of selling industrial chemicals.

After the plan for massive and simultaneous change was announced to a group of managers, including myself, one of the senior vice presidents asked if anyone had any questions or concerns. Everyone in the room was concerned about implementing so many drastic changes at once, and one of the more respected mid-level managers very tactfully voiced some concerns. The senior vice president responded by accusing him of not being a team player. The mid-level manager sheepishly sat down, not another word was said, and the plan was implemented.

Immediately after implementation, sales and profits began falling rapidly. According to the consultants and the new company leaders, this was expected because of the *hockey stick* effect.

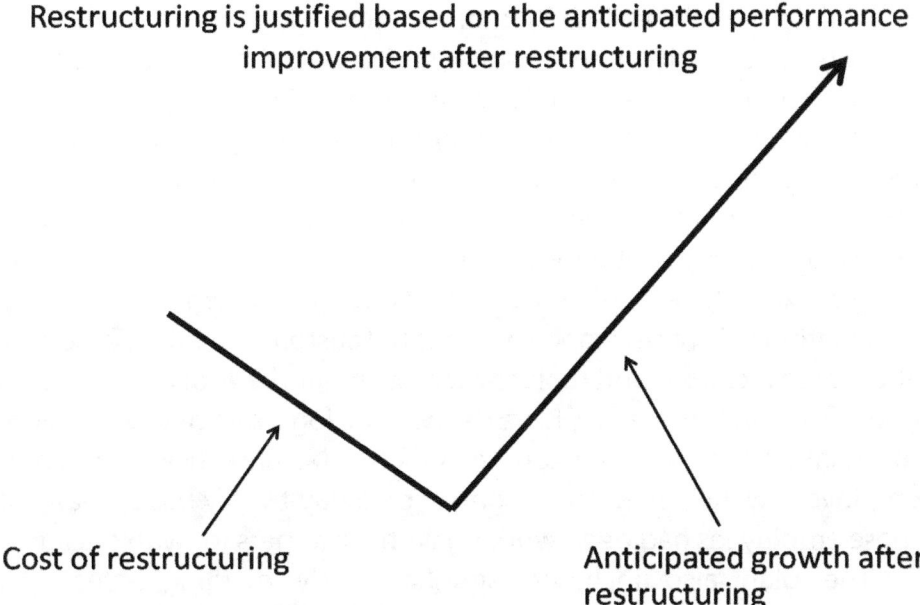

The "Hockey Stick" justification
Restructuring is justified based on the anticipated performance improvement after restructuring

Cost of restructuring

Anticipated growth after restructuring

Most employees felt that the downward trend was a very serious problem that had no short-term solution. Many of the real problems were associated with the strategies that were being implemented. First, anytime you're tinkering with something, it is best to make one adjustment at a time and determine the cause and effect (any entry-level mechanic knows this). If an automobile mechanic adjusts the timing, the carburetor, the valves, the transmission, various sensors, and the computer chip all at the same time, it is hard to say what helped and what did not help. Second, it is best to get as much advice from people who have actual experience with any existing issues before proceeding with any changes.

The chemical distribution company had been a consistent moneymaker, and since it was not operating poorly, it probably only needed continuous fine-tuning. There are times when organizations are on life support and radical restructuring is required (several U.S. automakers are currently in such a position), however, in many cases the Restructuring to Restructure decisions remind me of a surgeon who immediately decides to cut off a patient's leg to cure an infected toe without seeking another opinion. Because these surgeons have the authority, they perform the procedure and then pay themselves handsomely for it, even if the patient (organization) is now severely handicapped or even deceased. In the case of the chemical distribution company the changes were drastic and nonreversible and created many problems to overcome.

For example the plan was to centralize customer service by terminating (with a severance package) all customer service personnel at the field locations and replace them with hundreds of employees in one office. While there may have been sound logic behind the decision, the relationships with customers suffered because the terminated employees were closest to customers on a day-to-day basis. Many of these employees had been working with customers for with decades.

The plan also included simultaneously dividing sales and operations into two completely separate units. Because local branch managers had great rapport with customers, they knew how to service all of the customers in a territory and keep them as happy as possible with limited assets. Rearranging shipments and calling customers was a daily exercise because the capacity of the trucks and facilities were constantly tested. Under the new system there was little rhyme or reason as to who got serviced when, and because operations and sales were now so far removed from each other, there was no sense of urgency. Needless to say this also upset a tremendous number of customers and there was no easy fix for the problem.

The plan included further dividing the industrial chemical sales force into three newly created customer segments. Again while his may have seemed logical it was actually chaotic because each new sales force all sold basically the same chemicals, but now crisscrossed the country in a hundred different ways. This change coupled with the separation of sales and operations also created an environment where it was not possible to determine what areas of the company were profitable or non-profitable.

In order to reduce costs facilities would be shut down and everything would be moved into one location for a specific geography. The problem here was that the permits required to manage hazardous waste took two to ten years to modify for a new location, and the requirements conflicted with permits required to manage food grade and industrial chemicals. Management was so intent on implementing the plan that their answer to these unsolvable problems was to tell us to simply find a way to get it done.

One final piece to the plan was to ensure managers were well rounded by requiring almost all promotions to involve managers taking over a business unit that was completely different from the one they had previously managed. A little cross training of leaders is good; however switching nearly 100 percent of an organization's leadership created an environment where everyone seemed to be working for someone with little in depth knowledge about the business they were managing.

When I left the chemical distribution company, I had avoided the chaos by keeping our business intact. Our return on investment was over 40 percent and the rest of the chemical distribution businesses totaled only a few percent. This feat was even more amazing given that fact the chemical distribution industry was relatively strong, while the environmental industry we were competing in was in a severe recession. Even so, senior leadership kept insisting we restructure even if it negatively impacted our business.

As it turned out, the anticipated hockey stick effect was reversed for the chemical distribution company and the downward performance lasted for many years before any upward trend occurred. The hockey stick was reversed because so many changes were implemented simultaneously and little employee input was considered. Gradual improvements using high levels of employee input would have no doubt been far less painful.

Actual results of "restructuring to restructure" are frequently a reverse "Hockey Stick"

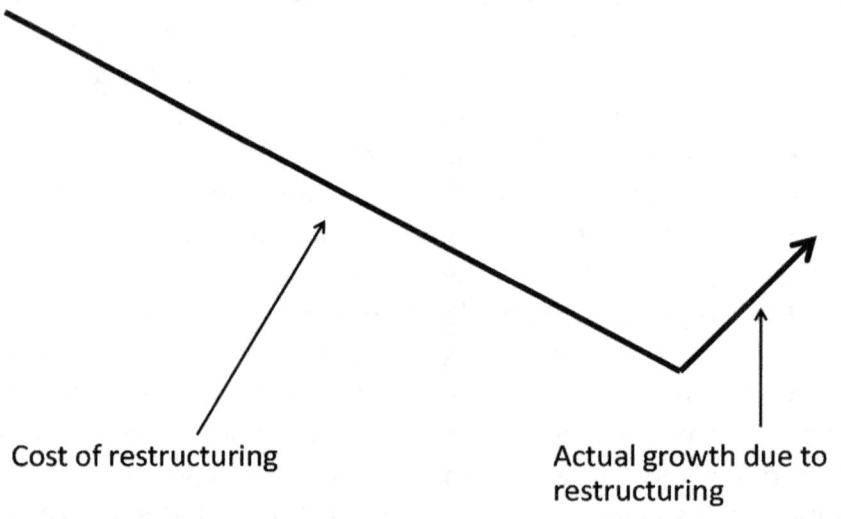

Cost of restructuring

Actual growth due to restructuring

Because long-term investment and returns are less of an option today, it seems that many organizations in this country are caught in a trap of ongoing Restructuring to Restructure. By frequently and dramatically changing leaders and strategies every few years, companies have experienced decades of hockey sticks and reverse hockey sticks with little real growth. When I joined my second environmental company, it was on its third major restructuring in only five years and since then it has been through several more.

Consequently, their performance had become a series of hockey sticks because of the continual restructuring.

Downward cycle of "restructuring to restructure"

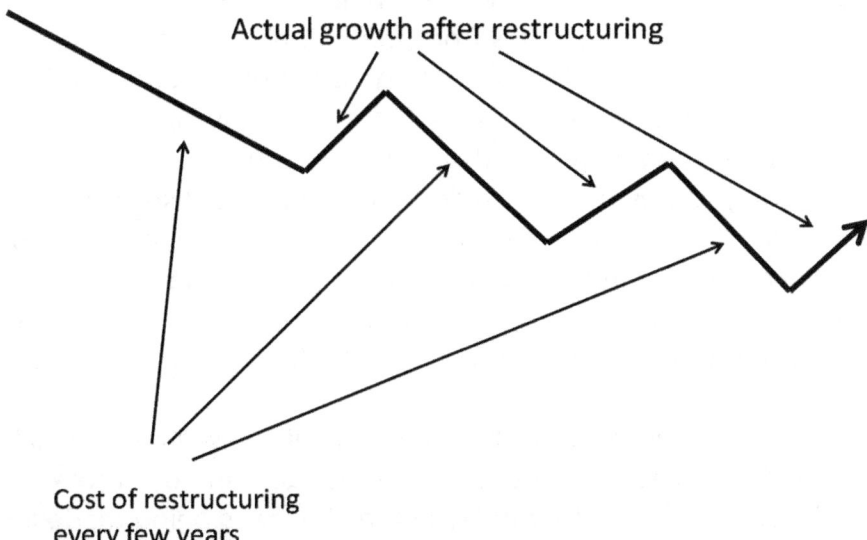

Actual growth after restructuring

Cost of restructuring every few years

Since the 1990s, many employees I talk to seem to be frustrated by the ever-changing Restructuring to Restructure leadership. It is interesting that I never seem to hear or read about continual major restructuring occurring (and the associated employee frustration) at successful companies like Honda, Toyota, Wegman's, Southwest Airlines, and Target.

Restructuring to Restructure Leadership Is Not Confined to CEOs
Not only can any manager fall into the trap of Restructuring to Restructure leadership, it is a natural tendency for new leaders at all levels of organizations to quickly implement many changes with little input from employees. Instead of devoting time to learning the

responsibilities, goals, and concerns of each employee within their group, new leaders frequently propose and implement sweeping changes with little input or understanding of the consequences. Immediately proposing to change the name of a department or business unit is usually a sign of Restructuring to Restructure leadership.

Unfortunately for industries like manufacturing, this type of leadership is a step backwards from traditional leadership. At least traditional leadership didn't waste huge amounts of organizational energy in continual restructuring and reorganizing, and the longer-term strategies required by manufacturing were accepted. Restructuring to Restructure leaders frequently act like everything done before their arrival was wrong. This is generally impossible because the organization would have not been able to survive if everything was incorrect before their arrival. New leaders need to ask many questions and learn as much as possible before implementing changes.

There is a simple litmus test to determine if a new strategy will be considered restructuring for the sake or restructuring by employees. If employees do not *understand* why the change is being made and they do not *buy into* the new strategy, then the new plan is most likely will be perceived as Restructuring to Restructure. The goal is to evolve without a lot of drama. Drama is created by leaders who change on a whim without employee input and a tremendous amount of organizational energy is wasted on drama. *People are actually not afraid of change* - they simply want their input heard and need to understand why they are changing. I have recently been working with Ron Hughes with Lighting Resources who has made significant changes to his organization without much drama. Ron calls the changes "an inclusive journey for all employees."

In 2009 the National Football League is a microcosm of what is happening to business leadership within the United States. Many years ago coaches generally won by imposing their will upon players much like the traditional leadership model. Teams blessed with more resources were continually more successful in the same way the United States experienced success during the 1900's because of our superior resources.

Competition among NFL teams began to increase due to free agency and salary caps and more parity came into the league. This is equivalent to the new increased global competition that has created more parity in the world. Over time, the NFL teams that adopted a more stable and employee oriented *leadership model* like Pittsburgh, Indianapolis, and New England have continued to succeed by utilizing input and gaining buy in from players and coaches.

Surprisingly a new trend has begun to develop in the NFL where suddenly there is less parity in the league due to *leadership styles*, and not the employees (players). The increased competition created by player parity pushed teams like Washington and Oakland to adopt a top down Restructuring to Restructure leadership style in an attempt to quickly turn things around. This has caused these teams to fall into somewhat of a death spiral of hired and fired coaches and often traded big name free agents. In stark contrast, the continuity of systems and leadership for the elite NFL teams today are so strong they have been able to successfully withstand coaching changes in Pittsburgh and Indianapolis, and even an injured star quarterback in New England.

This is exactly what is happening to many American organizations. In reaction to the increased global competition and world parity these companies also adopted top down Restructuring to Restructure leadership styles in an attempt to quickly turn their fortunes around. These organizations are also in somewhat of a death spiral of hired and fired leaders, ever changing strategies, and consequently burned out employees and customers. In contrast, organizations who utilize a long-term and stable employee oriented approach like Honda, Toyota, Wegman's, or Southwest Airlines, continue to refine their systems, *and they also continue winning.*

Rarely does a dramatic top down strategy produce long-term results. I recently listened to a speech given by Jeff Blashill, head coach of the Indianapolis Ice hockey team. Jeff coaches the best players in

North America in the 16 to 20 year old age group. These players are either destined for the NHL or top college programs. The Indianapolis Ice returned only four players from the previous year and Jeff was a rookie head coach. His team was picked to finish at the bottom of the 20 plus teams in North America. Instead the Indianapolis Ice won the championship. Jeff said their win had nothing to do with a single sweeping change. Their championship required input and dedication from all players and coaches and was the culmination of 1,000 steps towards success.

Chapter 27
Engaged and Effective Employees - Not Zombies

Successful organizations today are about <u>effectiveness</u> as opposed to busyness!

Leaders and employees are all in this together as <u>one team</u>!

Organizations have always been a delicate balance between employees, systems, procedures, and operations. They key to successful organizations will always be the balance between being effective versus being busy, and it is up to leaders to find this equilibrium. In the new global economy it is becoming more important that organizations marry employees systems, procedures, and operations to effectively produce products and services. Technology like e-mail, voice mail, and smart phones can make us more efficient, but can also make it easier than ever to fall into Drucker's activity traps.

One of the major problems with Restructuring to Restructure leadership is that it frequently produces lots of busyness with little effectiveness. With the use of a huge amount of input from engaged employees, new information systems can make companies dramatically more effective. The following are just a few of many possible examples:

- Trucking companies can use GPS to track their trucks to ensure routes are the most efficient, including calculating the amount of fuel to reach a stop with negotiated fuel prices.

- Stores now inventory everything automatically with bar code systems, allowing delivery from one large warehouse to replace exactly what was sold each day. This also eliminates labor costs associated with pricing and inventorying each item.

- Computerized manufacturing can improve quality and reduce costs.

Unfortunately these same powerful computer and information systems can also create busy environments where companies actually become less efficient. The following are examples where inefficiencies can occur:

Employees endlessly e-mail each other instead of resolving the matter with an actual discussion or meeting.

- I have worked with several sales organizations that have become very frustrated because their company eliminated customer service positions to save money. These companies provide a voice-automated greeting system and customers are shoved into voice mail hell. The end result is that sales personnel are on their smart phones most of the day doing customer service work via phone calls and e-mail instead of speaking face-to-face with prospective customers. In the end both the sales and customer service efforts suffer, and customers inevitably become frustrated.

- Employees also now have the ability with computers to produce endless reports that can be so complex they do not effectively serve anyone.

The most frightening area where U.S. leaders have failed to integrate employees, systems, and procedures in the new global economy is the manufacturing sector. As manufacturing facilities became less competitive due partly to the traditional top-down leadership philosophies, leaders reacted with Restructuring to Restructure leadership and simply shipped manufacturing jobs to other countries. The perception was that U.S. companies just could not compete with the cheaper labor of other countries. At the same time companies like Honda, Toyota, Mercedes, BMW and a huge number of their suppliers built very successful manufacturing facilities in the United States. They used American labor coupled with modern long-term leadership philosophies to successfully manufacture globally competitive products.

I am convinced that any country can compete successfully in many areas of the manufacturing segment provided organizations use the right leadership model and invest in their businesses long-term. Increased efficiencies from technology actually reduce the effect of higher labor costs allowing countries like the United States a better chance to compete. It does take a long-term commitment by leadership, and it does require a system of input and innovation from all employees to be successful. These are concepts that do not fit well with the new Restructuring to Restructure leadership.

The ultimate example of effective versus busy in recent years was demonstrated by Best Buy and Circuit City, the nation's two largest electronics retailers. Almost simultaneously these two organizations announced leadership changes that had little to do with their product or service offerings. In only a few short years, the difference in results was staggering:

Best Buy implemented a new policy allowing employees at corporate headquarters the freedom not to abide by set work hours - basically smashing the time clock and trusting its employees (Conlin, 2006). An employee's performance was measured by what he accomplished, not how many hours he sat in his office or cubicle. I understand that the same policies have been pushed down to stores as much as possible through flexible scheduling. Best Buy did not make this a major announcement; it was something it simply instituted and the word spread. Almost at the same time, in a classic Restructuring to Restructure leadership scenario, Circuit City announced to the world through press releases that it would reduce costs by eliminating its highest paid workers, starting with the sales force in each store (Associated Press, 2007). Anyone making over $12.00 an hour or so would be terminated.

Best Buys and Circuit City
Leadership decisions that impacted organizations

Best Buy
- Eliminated the time clock. Employees can come and go as they please. Focused on effectiveness and not busyness.

Circuit City
- Announced via press release they would increase profitability by terminating all their highest paid workers at their stores.

"You are one of our best, but you make over $12/hour, so you are fired!"

In the highly competitive retail electronics market, Best Buy increased productivity by 35 percent and reduced turnover by a whopping 50 percent. Unfortunately Circuit City did not fare as well. My son was working at Circuit City at that time while he was attending college. He was $.10 below the firing level for his department. Before the firing announcement he enjoyed his job, but afterward morale quickly disintegrated, and employees only cared enough to look busy until their shift was over. The message was clear: if you are effective and work hard, you will get promoted until you make enough to get fired. According to my son, in one Circuit City store in our area, everyone in the television department was terminated. The joke among remaining employees was that there was no one left in the store who could spell TV. Needless to say, customers were not impressed with the changes. In only a few years Circuit City filed for bankruptcy and is now out of business (Kavilanz, 2009). Best Buy is now the clear national leader for retail electronics, although with the new global economy they still have plenty of competition from myriad sources, including eBay, Amazon, Wal-Mart (both stores and online), and Overstocked.com.

Best Buys and Circuit City Results

Best Buy

- Productivity up 35%, employee turnover down 50%.

Circuit City

- Morale collapsed and they are now bankrupt and out of business.

I actually believe that if other companies would follow Best Buy's lead, they could significantly reduce the nation's energy problem. With employees effectively communicating by computer and phone, there is less need to drive in massive rush hour traffic and sit in the same building using phones and computers. If every organization adopted this policy, our energy consumption and greenhouse gas emissions would drop enormously. I also think Best Buy employees work harder because they know their employer trusts them. Trust, coupled with true measures of effectiveness, can help prevent zombies.

Chapter 28
Effective Leaders Are Humble Team Players - Not Royalty

There are certainly many strong business leaders in our country however the severe loss of our manufacturing base seems to indicate we can do better. In spite of the many books written that define the attributes of effective leaders as keeping their ego in check; listening to employee input; treating employees fairly; and recognizing and rewarding employees, much of American business leadership seems to struggle to demonstrate these traits. Chasing short-term financial returns simply does not allow American business leaders time to utilize these values successfully. Leaders promoted and sought after today charge in with risky top-down strategies ordering constant and dramatic change that may or may not benefit individual organizations short-term, however over time it negatively affects our entire economy because little of real value is being produced. I would almost equate this megatrend to a drug addict who will do anything to obtain a quick fix to feel better, even though in the long-term he is destroying himself.

So with all of the books filled with great leadership advice, why do so many leaders in this county not seem to get it? We continually read about leaders who seem to think they are royalty. They pay themselves absurd amounts of money even when their company is failing, make decisions similar to those at Circuit City that are clearly so short-term the organization will be severely damaged, or use the company's funds to pay for their own lavish lifestyle and perks. The only explanation seems to be the thirty year megatrend towards *fast money and consequently short-term leadership*.

There simply has to be more to leadership than:
- How can we put more dollars on the bottom line this month or quarter, even if we sacrifice our future?
- How can I completely restructure and disrupt the entire organization for the umpteenth time in the last several years to show that I am doing something?
- How can I, as a leader, add more zeros to my personal compensation, regardless of the ongoing success of the organization?

Effective leaders are humble team players (not royalty)

This is not to say that senior executives do not deserve to be paid well. Senior executives simply need to earn their money like everyone else, and their compensation should be based on the long-term performance of the company. All employees including senior executives have a duty to shareholders to earn the money they make and to spend the company's money effectively.

Executives of publicly owned companies who conspire with their boards to secure obscene amounts of money for themselves while the rest of the organization suffers are not only doing a disservice to shareholders, but they are contributing to the downward performance of the entire organization. Employees tend to shift to zombie behavior out of sheer frustration when they see this kind of selfish behavior by senior executives.

I was recently talking with an employee working the checkout line at one of the nation's largest home improvement stores, and our conversation turned to executive bonuses. She was still furious because their former CEO's contract required the company to essentially pay him $200 million dollars if the company decided to get rid of him because of poor performance. According to the cashier, her company actually paid the CEO $200 million to quit (Benner, 2007). She told me she felt this CEO was incredibly greedy to take the entire sum after he failed to perform. She felt there was nothing stopping him from taking perhaps $50 million and giving the rest back to the company. That CEO now heads up one of the nation's struggling car companies and my cashier told me she would never consider buying a car from that company.

Salaries and bonus information for publicly traded companies are public information, and consumers increasingly voice their discontent with companies whose executives pay themselves obscene amounts relative to their performance. If these executives are so sure that the benefits of a hockey stick dip in performance due to restructuring is such a good move, then they also should suffer during the downturn.

According to an article in *USA Today*, at least one CEO in Japan felt he should suffer along with his employees.

While Merrill Lynch's John Thain was splurging on a $1.2 million office makeover and Lehman Bros., Richard Fuld was drawing a $22 million bonus, the president of Japan Airlines was riding the bus to work, eating in the company cafeteria and cutting his salary to $98,000. 'I wanted to share the pain with my colleagues,' JAL president Haruka Nishimatsu, 61, says by e-mail (Wiseman & Jones, 2009).

I am sure there is no perfect guide for effective leaders, but some of the necessary traits are:
- Keeping their ego in check. Leaders are part of the team and need to act as such.
- Great listeners; believe there can never be too much input.
- Ambitious for the good of the team and themselves.
- Knowledgeable.
- Capable.
- Good all-around intelligence.
- Willing to take logical risks.
- Want to give recognition to others before themselves.
- Want to create a legacy by mentoring future effective leaders.

Early in *Leadership Essentials* (2005), Tom Peters listed contrasts using a word or a phrase to highlight what *was* and what *is*. A couple of these are very pertinent:

Was	Is
I don't care (what you think)	I don't know (all the answers)
Making a killing	Making a mark

In William E. Baker and Michael O'Malley's book *Leading with Kindness (2008)*, kindness is defined as a strength that successful leaders must exhibit. On page twenty-one is a very powerful and defining idea:

In order for companies to improve, the people of the organization have to become smarter and more resourceful and work together more effectively over time. For this to occur, people actually have to care about their work, the company, and one another. This requires the expert orchestration of a kind leader. (Baker, W., and O'Malley, M., 2008)

Probably the most profound thought on leadership is in Jim Collin's ground breaking book, *Good to Great (2001)*. In his book he defined the ultimate leader as a Level 5 Leader. In bold print on page 22, a Level 5 Leader is defined as:

Humility + Will =Level 5

I am personally still greatly influenced by my first exposure to business leadership. My first real boss was a foreman named Ed Smith at a very large Borg-Warner Chemicals plastics manufacturing facility. I worked there during the summers while going to college. Ed was a very nice, humble, and honest man, and his crew loved working for him. Ed did not raise his voice; however everyone knew who was in charge. Ed created a work family in which everyone looked out for each other. All of Ed's crew felt comfortable discussing any problems, issues, or ideas for improvement. Even though Ed's crew did not earn a penny more for their effort, they took tremendous pride in holding the record for producing the most resin in an eight-hour shift.

The Borg-Warner facility where we worked was unique in the Ohio River Valley. There were many large chemical manufacturing facilities along the river, but most of them were unionized, and workers punched time clocks. Borg-Warner was not unionized and there were no time clocks. The amazing part is that almost everyone showed up early! This allowed employees to meet with the previous crew to discuss issues and have a cup of coffee. Borg-Warner offered some of the best benefits and pay in the area, and all employees took safety and regulatory compliance very seriously. This was in the

1970s when safety and regulatory compliance was a low priority for many companies.

I worked summers at the Borg-Warner facility because my father worked for the company. Borg-Warner offered a program where employees' children who were attending college could work summers at the factory. They effectively used the college students to fill in for workers taking summer vacations. When my father heard I would be filling and stacking fifty-pound bags of gritty plastic resin in 90 degree, humid weather, on a swing shift that included working days, evenings, and nights, he told me I would find out why I was getting my college degree - so I never had to do that kind of work again. Instead, I still look upon those summers as one of my favorite work experiences because I was part of a work family, and we were accomplishing something significant and tangible every day. The job I was supposed to hate turned out to be one I loved.

My father always spoke very highly of Len Harvey, Borg-Warner's president at that time. My father had originally accepted a job with a fertilizer company in Chicago after college, but he left the company after a few years because it operated unethically by shorting farmers on the actual levels of nitrogen and other beneficial chemicals contained in the fertilizer. The fertilizer company would also send its trucks out grossly overweight and have them dodge scales. My father left to join Borg-Warner in 1959 and spent the rest of his career with the company. He always talked about how Len Harvey and the company constantly strove to do the right thing. One of Len Harvey's characteristics that amazed me was that he lived in the same small brick house in Vienna, West Virginia, even when he became president of the $4 billion Borg-Warner Chemical company.

I recently spoke with Len Harvey while he was visiting my father, both of whom are now retired. I asked Len, a very soft-spoken, highly intelligent person, what made him so successful? He thought for a minute and said, "I just wanted our people not to be afraid to make a mistake, and I wanted our people to try and do the right thing (L. Harvey, personal communication, 2008)." requirements.

When I consulted for Resin Recyclers, the president actually read every call report written by his sales people. Everyone in the organization felt comfortable talking to him about any areas in which they might improve. He, too, was a very humble yet driven individual.

I recently asked Bill Polian, president and general manager of the Indianapolis Colts what has made him so successful. Polian had just given a presentation during which he talked about how the organization places emphasis on drafting players of high integrity and character that fit in well with the organization. By sheer chance, I had moved to the Buffalo area in 1984, when the Bills were one of the worst teams in football and Polian had become their general manager. He built the Bills into a team that went to four straight Super Bowls. When I moved to Indianapolis in 1997, the Colts were also terrible, but Polian took over and built them into one of the best teams in football. During his presentation, Polian said that the Colts eliminate more players in the draft than most other team because they do not believe the player's character fits in with the Colts organization (B. Polian, public speech, 2008). If the Colts were going to win, it would be with outstanding individuals, not just outstanding talent.

After his presentation, I asked him how he accomplished these dramatic changes at multiple NFL organizations. He was incredibly humble and said, "Well, you just kind of have to get lucky and find a good coach and quarterback, and then build a team around them (B. Polian, personal communication, 2008)." The interesting aspect about Polian's philosophy is that, in an era of big names and free agency, the Colts never seem to pay huge money for big name free agents. They prefer to continue building their organizations by selecting players who fit their organization. Bill Polian builds great teams through continual refinement with players of high character. It is interesting to watch other teams that utilize Restructuring to Restructure leadership by constantly making sweeping changes in coaches, players, and strategies. These teams rarely approach the same level of success as the Colts.

Most of the time I speak with leaders who have built great organizations, I find them to be humble about what they accomplished. They create cultures in which employees are effective and enjoy going to work. This type of leader does not need to prove he is the boss; he is respected by employees because he is humble, he listens, and he works hard to do the right thing for everyone, and employees respond accordingly. The president of Resin Recyclers even attending the sales training sessions I conducted. In the same way the Colts choose players that fit their team, an organization full of humble team players can be continually reinforced through the interview process, employee reviews, and the language included in the Employee Induction Motor.

Although successful leaders are often humble, they are also very driven, and if you are around them very long, you find it takes hard work to implement an effective leadership system. Effective leaders can never stop listening and learning. It is interesting that if you ask a room full of leaders whether they have ever worked for a poor manager, most will raise their hands. If you ask the same group if they are a poor manager, few will raise their hands. There must be a disconnect somewhere. This is why effective leaders need to be humble and realize they can always improve their organizations and themselves. Leaders need to realize that they are not perfect and need to admit and learn from their mistakes. Employees respect that kind of attitude.

In my opinion it comes down to what I call the Leadership Paradox: *If a leader thinks they are a great leader, they almost certainly are not a great leader.* Leaders must instead strive to be an *ever-improving and effective leader.* *Effective leaders* recognize they do not have all the answers. *Effective leaders* create an environment of rewards, recognition, and feedback that allows all employees to provide continuous input for improvement.

Chapter 29
Summary

From 1978 to 1982, I was a sales representative for a chemical distribution company in central Illinois. I had a thick book that listed every business operating in the state organized by city, and eventually, I sought out each business in my territory. It always amazed me that someone was manufacturing something in almost every town - even places with a population of only a few hundred. I liked to tour their facilities because I wanted to see what chemicals they might be using, and I loved simply seeing how different products were manufactured.

A huge number of these facilities are now gone. If you search websites listing high paying jobs today, almost all of them are for health services, financial services, or Information technology - only a fraction of a percent are for manufacturing. The idea that America can no longer compete in manufacturing because labor is cheaper elsewhere and we are too regulated has created the perception that our only option is to become a service-based economy. In terms of manufacturing jobs it seems like Americans have simply quite trying. We are a country that has never quit at anything and yet when it comes to building goods we are, for perhaps the first time ever, becoming quitters.

Many other countries facing similar regulations and labor costs have not suffered the same fate as the United States. Business leaders in these countries recognize that a healthy economy needs to have a balance of service and manufacturing jobs since buying most manufactured goods from overseas creates a huge trade imbalance. In the United States we lost 5.3 million manufacturing jobs in the last decade and if the trend continues then in two decades essentially all American manufacturing jobs will be gone. At some point we have to ask ourselves what we are going to sell to a global economy to create wealth within our country to pay for all of the services being provided.

When I grew up in a small town in Southeastern Ohio, there were many large factories along the river that employed tens of thousands of workers. In town was a small hospital to provide medical care for the workers and their family. Today most of the manufacturing jobs are gone and now the greatly expanded hospital is the largest employer in the area. I can't help but wonder who pays for all of the health care when there are few jobs in the area that create value.

Another problem is that manufacturing creates innovation and if we resign ourselves to a service based economy one has to wonder if we can maintain our position as the world's superpower without also being a world leader in manufacturing and innovation. If we can shift to a more long-term and employee oriented strategy and leadership model like the Employee Induction Motor, I believe we can reclaim our position as the world leader in innovation and manufacturing.

The problem in our country is that we need to *buy American*, it is that we need to commit to the long-term strategies and investment it takes to *build competitive products in America*. Less sophisticated and more labor-intensive products will always be produced cheaper in developing countries in the same way Japan did in the 1950's and 1960's. However there will also always be a need for more expensive and sophisticated products where labor costs are less important that we can produce in the United States. Toyota, Honda, BMW, and their hundreds of suppliers have all been able to employ American workers and successfully build high quality products that can be exported anywhere in the world. The difference is that they have not given up on the American workforce and their leadership model is long-term and employee-oriented.

Since World War II, most parents have urged their children to go to college so they could obtain white collar jobs and do better than their generation. It also became a popular notion that it was good for our country for business leaders to get rich as quickly as possible. These trends are two major reasons why the United States is losing manufacturing jobs at such a high rate compared to industrialized countries with a similar cost of living. Leadership's thinking has become very shortsighted and blue collar jobs seem to be considered "undignified." This is not to say that wealth and education are not important; both are very important, but it is what a person does with his education and wealth that creates his legacy. Using wealth and education to help create good jobs in which Americans create great products and services is far more rewarding than simply gaining individual riches at the expense of others and the long-term success of our great country.

When I have talked about American business leaders being greedy for the short-term some people have told me that is the "American way." It is almost as if these people have accepted that many leaders have seemed to slip on a WWSD (What Would Scrooge Do?) bracelet. These leaders do not seem to care if they treat their employees like Bob Cratchet by paying themselves handsomely while they abuse customers and eliminate jobs and benefits for employees. It is very easy to find Scrooge like behavior in many corporations today: at the same time banking companies are paying obscene bonuses to their executives they are refusing to reduce 29.99% interest rates to strapped consumers who were forced to use credit cards due to job loss or unexpected health care costs; while health insurance executives are some of the highest paid in the country, babies are being denied coverage because they are a few pounds too heavy or too light; and a vaccine manufacturer injects a recalled vaccine into babies and does not consider contacting or even listening to parents of a child who became severely ill immediately after receiving the vaccine.

If children suffer the same fate as Tiny Tim was destined had Scrooge not changed his ways, so be it; all that is important is how rich these leaders and their organizations can become in the short-term. I do not believe this is the American way and business leaders need to realize that by utilizing employee input to develop strategies for the long-term best interests of their employees, customers, and organizations, the better their organizations will perform long-term.

Many Americans today are feeling unfulfilled, and the reason may be that the pursuit of education and wealth alone may not make them as happy as they anticipated. I think psychologists may tell you happiness comes more from what you accomplish. My father-in-law was one of the most happy and content people I have known in spite of the fact that he left school after the eighth grade to work on the family farm. He was very proud to talk about the roads he built during his career in construction. Those roads and his reputation as a good, honest, and hard-working family man are the legacies he has left behind. My father spent his career as an executive manufacturing strong plastics used to make phones, car grills, and even Lego's. As for me, I am very proud of providing services to properly manage hazardous waste and contribute to helping clean up our great country. Not only did I help reduce pollution for future generations, I also helped American industry continue to manufacture products by providing a safe and simple solution to dispose of chemical wastes.

I am also very proud of creating an organization of employees who enjoyed going to work every day, and I am proud to have always found time for my family. I cannot imagine how anyone could truly find happiness by simply gaining wealth at the expense of making employees' lives miserable, or by taking away almost all of their quality family time. I really believe the Employee Induction Motor provides a model to create long-term success and happiness for everyone.

In spite of losing massive numbers of manufacturing jobs, Americans work longer hours than other countries like Germany who produce far more products. This is probably because if little is actually being accomplished, then the only measurement of a worker is the time they are at work. When I worked at the chemical distribution company's headquarters it was very common for many of the 1,200 workers, who spent their entire day sitting in cubicles, in meetings, on the phone, or on their computer, to complain that they were too busy to take their vacation. The old saying, "The problem with doing nothing is that you don't know when you are done" seems to apply to many American workers.

I distinctly remember that all of the employees that conducted tours of their manufacturing facilities when I was a sales representative loved to show off their operations. Whether they were manufacturing car fuses or giant earth moving equipment, you could tell they were proud to make necessary products. I cannot imagine that they did not feel some fulfillment for what they were accomplishing every day.

Unfortunately, today there are far too many employees isolated in cubicles and spending the day e-mailing colleagues. They no doubt end each day wondering what they accomplished. Too many leaders and investors are focused on the very short term, and if a company misses its profit or revenue forecast by a penny, its stock takes a hit. Under these circumstances there is little incentive to invest in anything for the long-term. Too many employees are burned out but dare not seek fulfilling employment for fear of losing benefits that have now become a rare offering. Leaders feel they do not have time to obtain input from employees before implementing the next round of restructuring or reorganization.

This is not to say that the United States is without strong business leaders. There are still many leaders who are providing for the future of their companies. These individuals understand that it takes effective, engaged employees to create a successful organization. To be successful in a global economy, the goal is to create an organization full of effective employees and obtain more input from employees not less. The following chart demonstrates the differences between the three leadership styles described in this book:

Future Leadership Model - EIM

	Traditional Leadership	"Restructuring to Restructure"	Future Leadership - EIM
Leadership style	Top Down	Top Down	Participate and oversee a structured organization, acting as one team, to continually improve
Employee input and "buy-in"	Some	Little or none	As much as is possible
Organizational and other changes	Not very frequent or dramatic	Dramatic and frequent	Generally continual refinements

    I am sure that the Employee Induction Motor is not the only way to improve innovation and productivity within an organization. We do know that it has consistently lead to record results in all areas in almost every organization in which we have applied the concept. Regardless of what type of industry or business you are in, the Employee Induction Motor utilizes input and reward/recognition/feedback to release the power of an entire workforce. Input with corresponding recognition and reward creates innovation, and the United States has traditionally been a nation of innovators who believe that when working as a team, we can accomplish anything.

    One of the goals we established when we created the Employee Induction Motor is that it would fit on one page or one poster and be easily understood by all employees. It is also easily customized to any organization, and works with current improvement and HR programs (the top and bottom arrows). It is designed to benefit any organization and I hope it will provide ideas to power your organization.

Summary

The Employee Induction Motor fits on one page or one poster

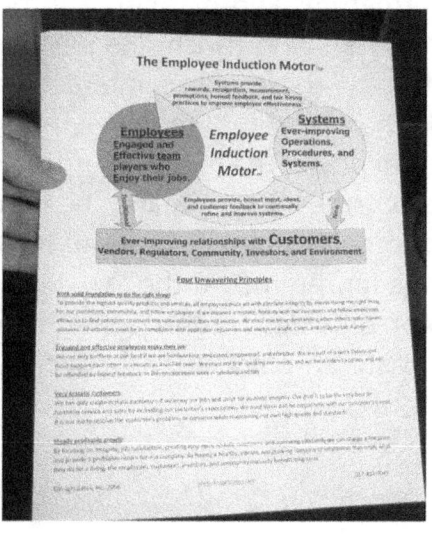

- EIM <u>complements</u> continuous improvement programs and human resources programs.

- The <u>same message</u> applies to employees, customers, regulators, the community.

- Can be <u>understood by every employee</u> in the organization.

- Can be <u>customized</u> for any organization.

From a personal perspective, I believe the Employee Induction Motor is also a good model to follow as an individual. If you adopt this as your own, even if your organization does not, it will help you succeed in your career long-term both financially and personally. It is a great guide to post at your desk to stay focused on the objectives that will help you succeed.

I have probably known as many wealthy people who seemed unhappy as I have happy and satisfied people of more modest wealth (Futrelle, 2006). In the end it is about what you accomplish in your career, your family, and your life that creates your legacy. From a business perspective, doing the right thing to create long-term sustainable and substantial products and services, to gainfully employ effective and productive workers, to create ecstatic customers, and to create long-term financial success, will always be far more rewarding.

Perhaps within our small environmental business we stumbled upon something close to the basic building blocks for all business organizations. Perhaps Employees and Systems are the foundation of all businesses similar to the way armatures and magnets are the basic parts that make up electric motors. And much like electric motors, there is a delicate balance to how these pieces interact, as demonstrated by the Employee Induction Motor. Employee input and recognition are the two currents that power the model in order to meet the demands of customers and outside influence, and the four unwavering principles are the laws of physics when it comes to how an organization needs to behave in the long-term. At the very least, I hope the Employee Induction Motor provides leaders something to think about in terms of how to create an efficient and effective business organization.

Acknowledgments

First and foremost, I would like to recognize the many leaders I have had the privilege of working for, and learning from, during my career, including Dick Hunter, Tom Henehan, Fred Fehsenfeld Jr., Rudolf Zeangerle, John McCarthy, Jim Lupo, Tom King, Ken Price, and Ron Hughes. I would especially like to acknowledge Ed Smith, my first boss when I worked at Borg-Warner Chemical, who demonstrated to me that nice guys can finish first. I would also like to acknowledge Len Harvey, the president of Borg-Warner at that time, for his kind, intelligent, and driven leadership that infused the entire organization.

I would like to acknowledge my fellow employees who helped build one of the most profitable and successful environmental businesses during the 1990s, including Larry Eidy, Cathy Wiles, Jeff Kirk, Scott Bult, Jack Sweet, Mike Maier, Allison King, Craig Stanley, Bill Fitzsimmons, Walt Billings, Ed McMahon, and David Proud.

I would like to acknowledge other people that I looked to as mentors, including Tom Jungjohann, Tom Dressel, Ron Gates, and Jim Hackathorn.

I am extremely grateful to Marvin Dufner, Ray Kohout, Tom, Doug, and Donnie Wise, Kevin Prunsky, and Ron Hughes for allowing me a chance to start a career in consulting and speaking.

Other business people I have admired include Pete Septoski, Bill Hancock, Craig Harper, Steve Talley, Keith Zimcosky, Bob O'Brien, Dean Nardi, Dave Lusk, John Georgagi, Eddie Lancaster, Alan McKim, Darci Ackerman, John Lucks, John Corcia, Dave Manley, Jeff Blashill, John Faurote, Stacey Smallwood, Bill McDaniel, Joe Chalhoub, Joe Wesel, Scott Cronk, Tina Woods, Steve MacDonnell, Gary Rabine, Dave Homeyer, and Troy Gamble.

I would like to acknowledge the organizations I have had the privilege of working for either as en employee or a consultant. In order to maintain confidentiality I have created fictitious companies and examples based on my experiences.

I would like to thank Bowling Green State University for accepting me and for providing four years of education and life experiences.

I would like to acknowledge Red Adams and Aunt Edie for providing an example of how to enjoy life, and I would like to thank all of our family and friends who have made our lives so fulfilling.

I would like to thank Gary Meyer for help filing all the proper paperwork to actually start a business and for assisting with data research within the Bureau of Labor and Statistics. And thank you also to the super models on the cover, John Knight, Tim Knight, Niki Walsh, and Brittany Knight, and for John Faurote's help with the cover graphics. I would also like to thank Jon Chase for his advice on occasion.

I would especially like to thank Nicole Walsh for her help editing and finalizing this book. This book is a far better effort due to Niki's excellent editing. I would also like to thank Bob Pegan, and Kim Hargrove for their honest feedback when they first read the manuscript for the book.

I would also like to acknowledge all of my fellow Magic Castle Cart volunteers at Riley Hospital for Children, especially Bob Baxter and Steve Kellam, who developed the idea and have spoiled kids at Riley's for several hours per week for over a decade.

I especially want to thank all the readers of this book and all my past and future clients who have allowed me to work with their organizations.

References

1. Pfizer. (2009). *A pioneering spirit on the frontiers of medicine.* Retrieved August 19, 2009, from the Pfizer website http://www.pfizer.com/
2. Mullen, Mike. (2009). *Speech.* National Student Leadership Conference. American University, Washington D.C. 6 April 2009.
3. Olsen, B., & Cabadas, J. (2002). *American auto factory.* St. Paul, MN: MBI Publishing Company.
4. Gardner, H. (1993). *Frames of mind: the theory of multiple intelligences.* New York: Basic Books.
5. Makower, J. (1994). *Beyond the bottom line: Putting social responsibility to work for your business and the world.* New York: Simon & Schuster.
6. Snyder, A. (2008). *CDS Market is a $50 trillion blind date from hell.* Retrieved August 19, 2009 from Contrarian Profits website at http://www.contrarianprofits.com/.
7. Sherwood, A. (1986). *Breakpoints: making career stages work for you.* Garden City, NY: Doubleday Publishing Group.
8. Grubbs-West, L. (2005) *Lessons in loyalty: how Southwest Airlines does it – an insider's view.* Dallas, TX: Cornerstone Leadership Institute.
9. Bertsch, K. A., & Mann, C. (2005) Title.*CEO Compensation and Credit Risk.* Retrieved August 19, 2009 from the Moody's website http://www.moodys.com/
10. Reitman, I., & Simmons, M. (Producers), & Landis, J. (Director). (1978). *National Lampoon's Animal House* [Motion Picture]. United States: Universal Pictures.
11. Futrelle, D. (2006). *Can Money Buy Happiness?* Retrieved from Money Magazine website at http://money.cnn.com/.

12. Mayo, Elton. (1949). *Hawthorne and the Western Electric Company, the social problems of an industrial civilization.* New York, NY: Routledge.
13. Coy, Peter. (2009). *The Lost Generation.* Retrieved November 18, 2009, from the Business Week website http://www.businessweek.com/
14. Bureau of Labor Statistics. (2009). *Occupation employment statistics.* Retrieved August 19, 2009 from BLS website http://www.bls.gov/.
15. Bureau of Labor Statistics. (2009). *Employee benefits in the United States.* Retrieved August 19, 2009 from BLS website http://www.bls.gov/.
16. U.S. Census Bureau. (2007). *U.S. international trade in goods and services.* Retrieved August 19, 2009 from U.S. Census website http://www.census.gov.
17. Moberg, D. (2009). *Give CEO pay the pink slip.* Retrieved August 19, 2009 from In These Times website http://www.intesetimes.com.
18. U.S. Government Accountability Office. (2005). *Offshoring of services: an overview of the issues.* Retrieved August 19, 2009 from U.S. Government Accountability Office website http://www.goa.gov.
19. Davis, R. (1994). *The gift of dyslexia.* New York, NY: Perigee trade.
20. Wright, C. (Host). (2007). *The brain game.* In television show Brain Game. Butler, IN: WTHR.
21. Immelt, J. (2009). *2008 GE Annual report.* Retrieved August 19, 2009, from General Electric website http://www.ge.com/
22. Drucker, P. (1954). *Practice of management.* New York: HarperCollins Publishers.
23. Ohio History Central (2009). *Cuyahoga river fire.* Retrieved August 19, 2009, from the Ohio History Central website http://www.ohiohistorycentral.org/
24. Jensen, T. (2002). *Cheating: an inside look at the bad things good NASCAR Winston Cup racers do in pursuit of speed.* Phoenix, AZ: David Bull Publishing.

References

25. Holm, B. (2009). *Blowing up Pepsi.* Retrieved August 19, 2009, from the Business Week website http://www.businessweek.com/
26. Conlin, M. (2006). *Smashing the clock: Inside Best Buy's radical reshaping of the workplace.* Retrieved August 19, 2009, from The MSNBC website http://www.msnbc.msn.com/
27. Associated Press. (2007). *Circuit City to fire more than 3,400 workers: retailer will replace them with new employees paid at market-based rate.* Retrieved August 19, 2009, from the MSNBC website http://www.msnbc.msn.com/
28. Kavilanz, P. (2009). *Circuit City to shut down: Court approves bankrupt electronics retailer's motion to liquidate and close its remaining 567 stores.* Retrieved August 19, 2009 from the CNN Money website http://money.cnn.com/
29. Peters, T. (2005). *Leadership.* New York: DK Publishing, Inc.
30. Baker, W., & O'Malley, M. (2008). *Leading with kindness: how good people consistently get superior results.* New York: AMACOM.
31. Collins, J. (2001). *Good to Great: Why some companies make the leap...and others don't.* New York: HarperCollins Publishers.
32. Dungy, T. (2007). *Quiet strength: the principles, practices, and priorities of a winning life.* Wheaton, IL: Tyndale House Publishers.
33. Ahlrichs, N. (2000). *Competing for talent: key recruitment and retention strategies for becoming an employer of choice.* Palo Alto, CA: Consulting Psychologists Press, Inc.
34. Weisenthal, J. (2009). *$1.2 million spent to redecorate Thain's office.* Retrieved August 19, 2009, from the Business Insider website http://www.businessinsider.com/
35. Benner, K. (2007). *Robert Nardelli named CEO of Chrysler.* Retrieved August 19, 2009 from the CNN Money website http://money.cnn.com/
36. Wiseman, P. & Jones, D. (2009). *In Japan, more CEOs share the pain of tough times.* Retrieved from the USA Today website http://www.usatoday.com/

www.ingramcontent.com/pod-product-compliance
Lightning Source LLC
Chambersburg PA
CBHW071423170526
45165CB00001B/373